DATE DUE 6/17

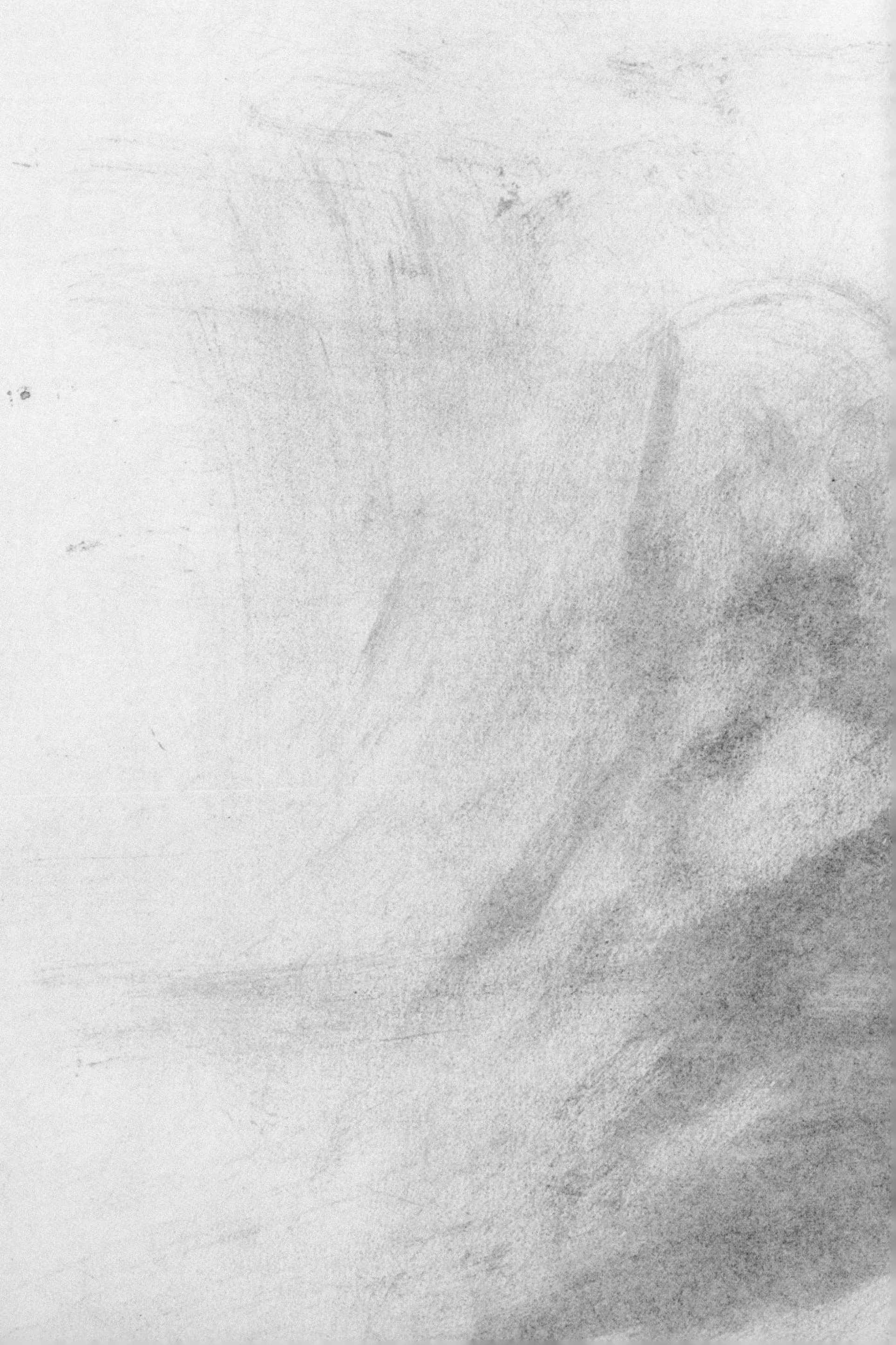

Praise for Graham Roumieu's previous book IN ME OWN WORDS.

"Brilliantly funny."
San Francisco Chronicle

"So freaking funny you'll be out of breath."
Salon.com

ABOUT THE CREATOR

This is Graham Roumieu's second book.
It was poorly researched.

www.roumieu.com

PLUME
Published by Penguin Group
Penguin Group (USA) Inc., 375 Hudson Street, New York, New York 10014, U.S.A.
Penguin Group (Canada), 90 Eglinton Avenue East, Suite 700, Toronto, Ontario, Canada M4P 2Y3
(a division of Pearson Penguin Canada Inc.)
Penguin Books Ltd., 80 Strand, London WC2R 0RL, England
Penguin Ireland, 25 St. Stephen's Green, Dublin 2, Ireland (a division of Penguin Books Ltd.)
Penguin Group (Australia), 250 Camberwell Road, Camberwell,
Victoria 3124, Australia (a division of Pearson Australia Group Pty. Ltd.)
Penguin Books India Pvt. Ltd., 11 Community Centre, Panchsheel Park, New Delhi – 110 017, India
Penguin Books (NZ), cnr Airborne and Rosedale Roads, Albany,
Auckland 1310, New Zealand (a division of Pearson New Zealand Ltd.)
Penguin Books (South Africa) (Pty.) Ltd., 24 Sturdee Avenue, Rosebank,
Johannesburg 2196, South Africa

Penguin Books Ltd., Registered Offices: 80 Strand, London WC2R 0RL, England

First published by Plume, a member of Penguin Group (USA) Inc.

First Printing, December 2005
10 9 8 7 6 5 4 3 2 1

ISBN 0-452-28685-9

Printed in Mexico
Designed by Chrystal Falcioni and Graham Roumieu

Me Write Book

It Bigfoot Memoir

graham roumieu

A PLUME BOOK

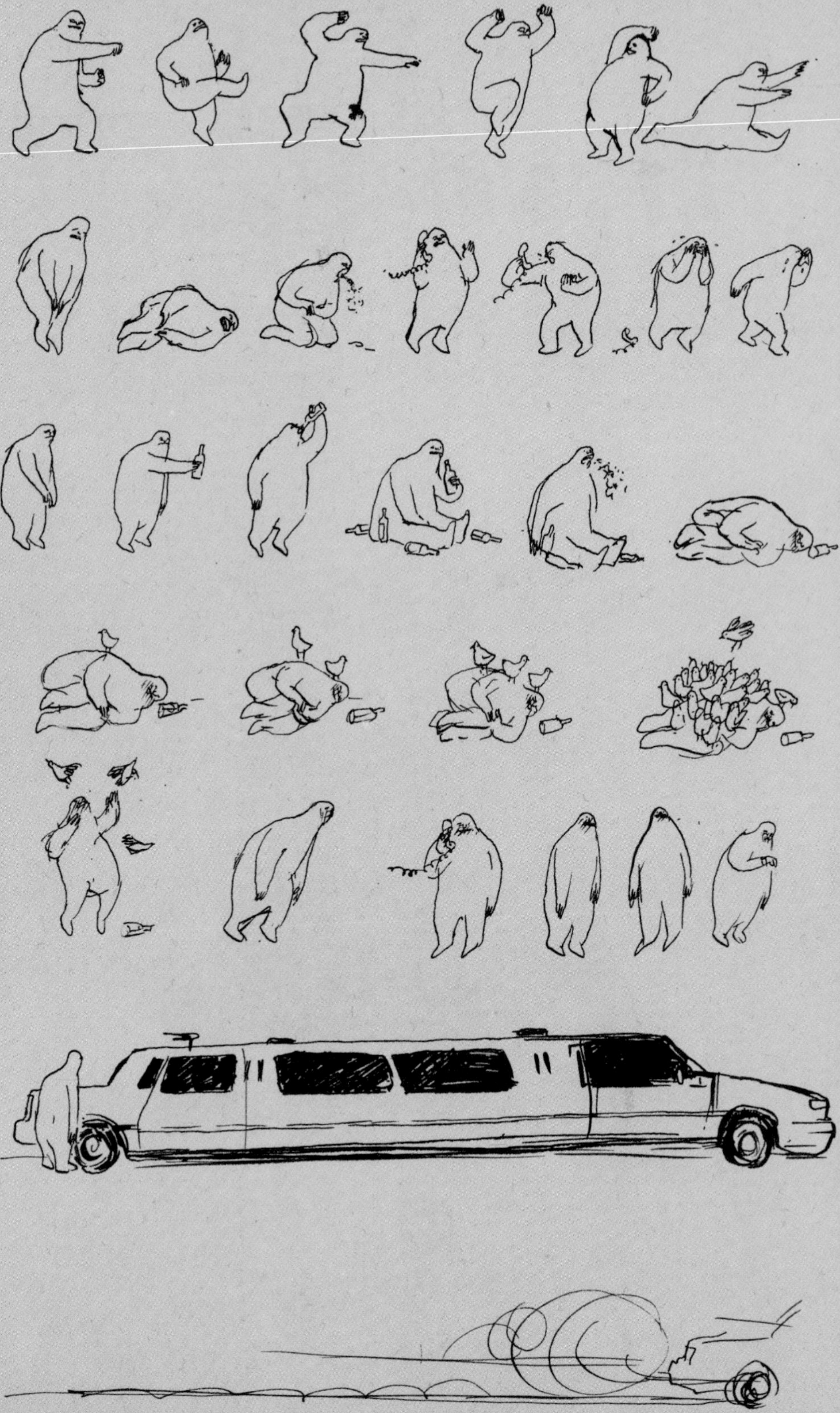

Bigfoot want
thank fans.
~~You like a rainbow~~
~~in Hell.~~

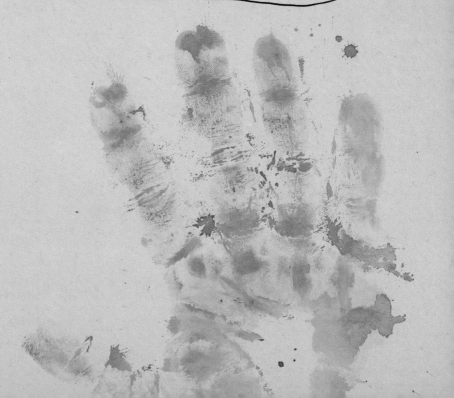

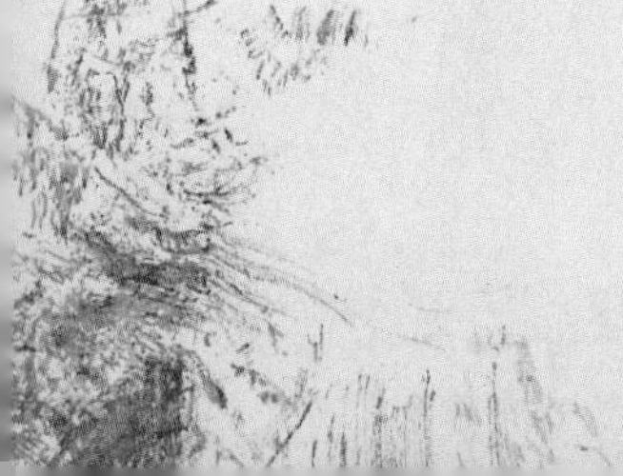

Introduction by

Mr. Loch Ness Monster

of

Loch Ness,
Scotland

Oh, hello!

Some time ago now I was doing a lot of media appearances but it just got a bit much with all the tabloids and the paparazzi. Constant hounding with all the cameras and the questions and the sonar and the wee submarines and whatnot. I know what it's like to put yourself out there. Back in the day, Bigfoot and I chummed around quite a bit, shooting the breeze and getting into all kinds of shit. But frankly I'm a little surprised he asked me to do this introduction for him.

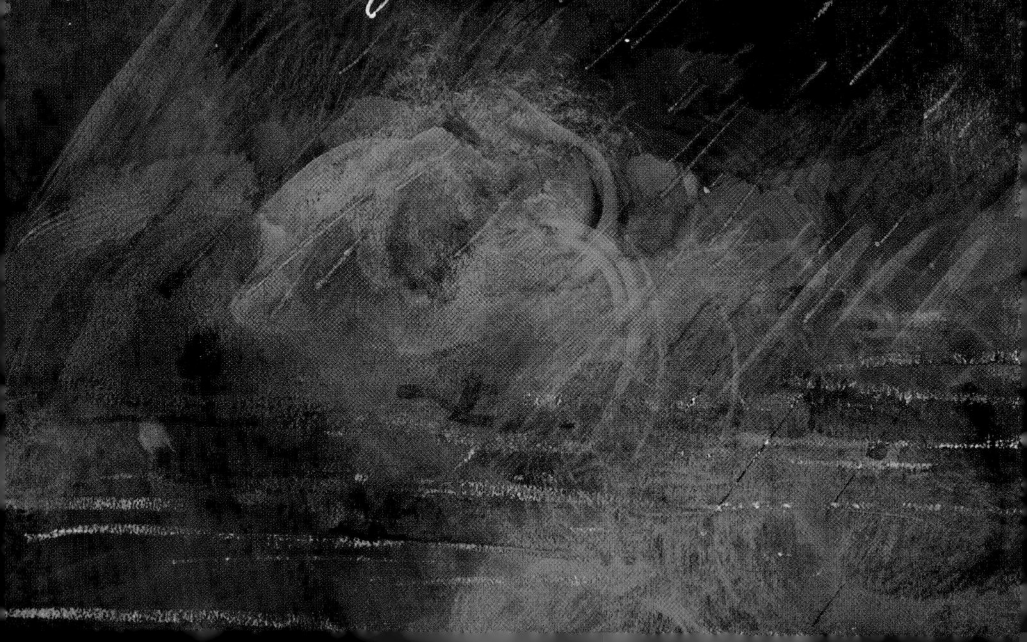

It's been awhile since we've spoken.

I guess it's my fault

I mean I kind of dropped out.

Just been doing a lot of sleeping, listening to the latter records of Brian Wilson.

Just kind of floating.

But I was struck when I first read this book, it's really good shit. It reminds us all that there's someone else out there dealing with the isolation, the terrible blurry photos, being hunted and all the other dark, cold, lonely things that feed great art. Some of it is a bit much though; I'll never understand the woodsy thing and I'm pretty sure I don't have feet.

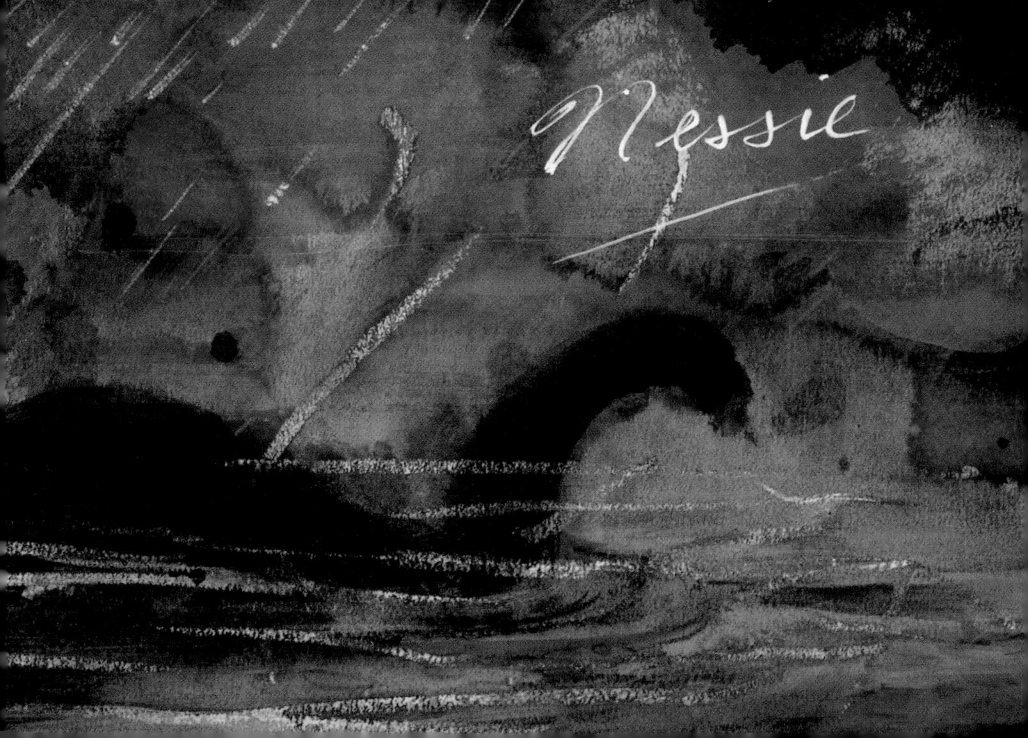
Nessie

Me Write Book

Stink

Yes, everyone know Bigfoot smell like shit. Please make effort not to point out every time you see Bigfoot.
Thank you

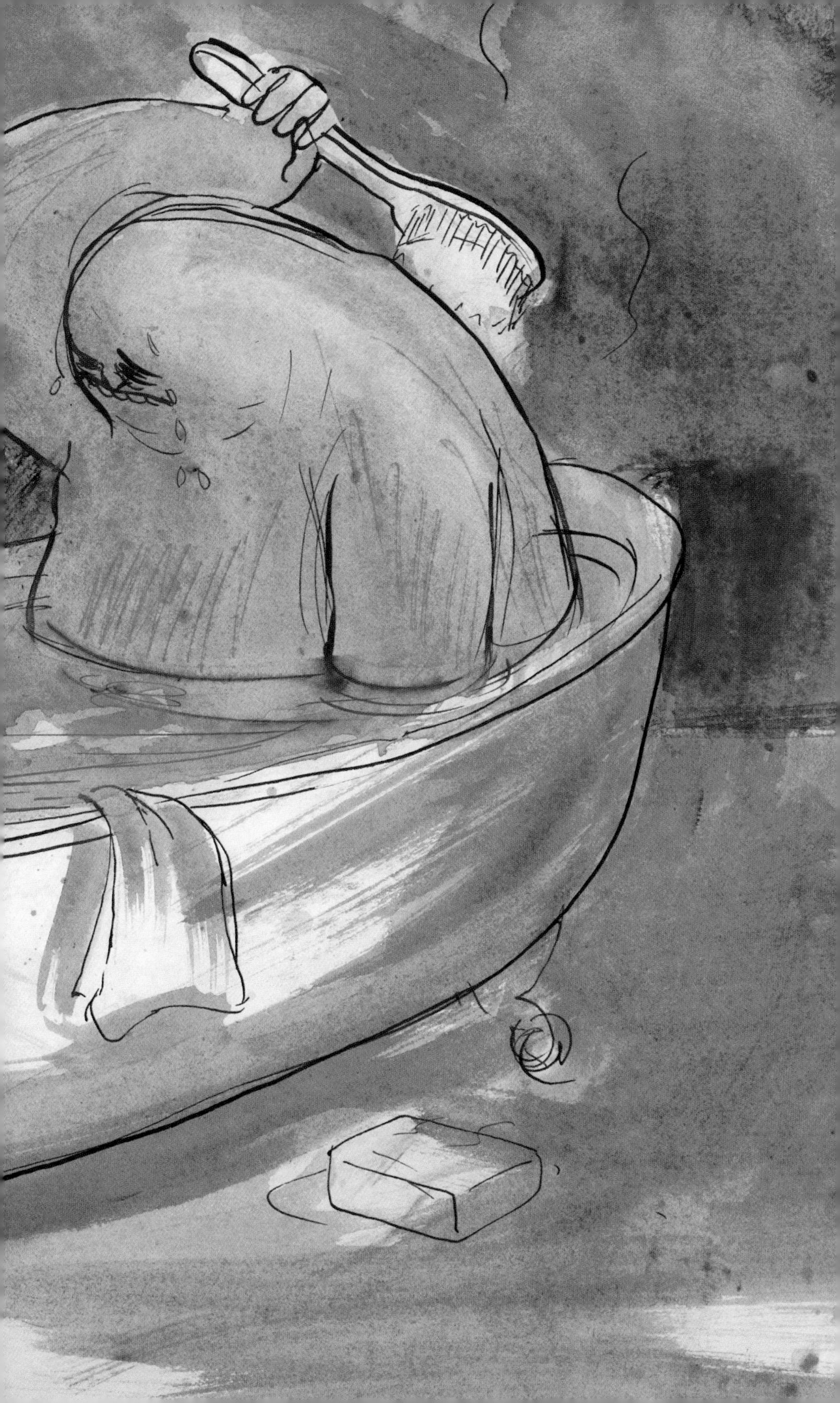

Fall

It true, Bigfoot career been in hole lately. Bigfoot mania of 70's and 80's nothing but distant memory. I famous for ability to not be see but don't think I not notice you not notice. I blame music television and internet. People too lazy and stupid to appreciate conceptual artist like Bigfoot who appeal is absence. If Bigfoot give stuff away like santa I be everybody hero. ~~With thought like this I wrote for T.V. show Northern Exposure.~~

Santa is fat, pandering bastard.

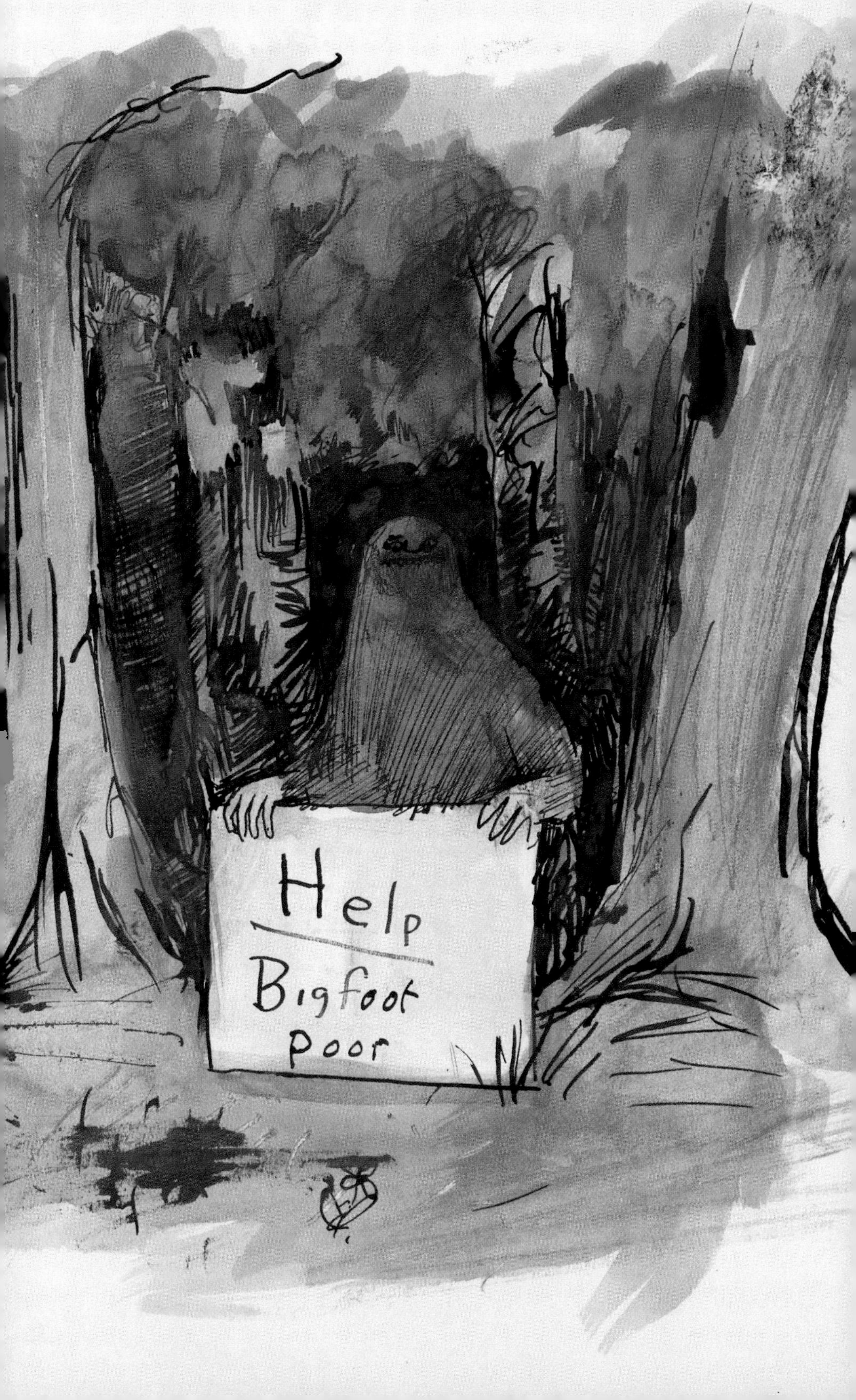
Help
Bigfoot
poor

All Gone

Have to admit Bigfoot live
pretty high on hog. When career
going good money no object,
Throw crazy party for A-list friends
every night of week. Morris
the Cat, Andrew Dice Clay
and Emilo Estevez. We rip it up
like the care free, young god
we was. Fog of fame obscure
reality, no accountable.
Andy D. kill 3
hobo. He call judge's mom awful thing
during trial. Jury think it fresh
and funny and aquit him. Madness.
But our fortune, like our fame,
fleeting. Have not talk those

guys in years. Assume they dead. Still, would not trade those day for anything.

Nature Vs Nurture.

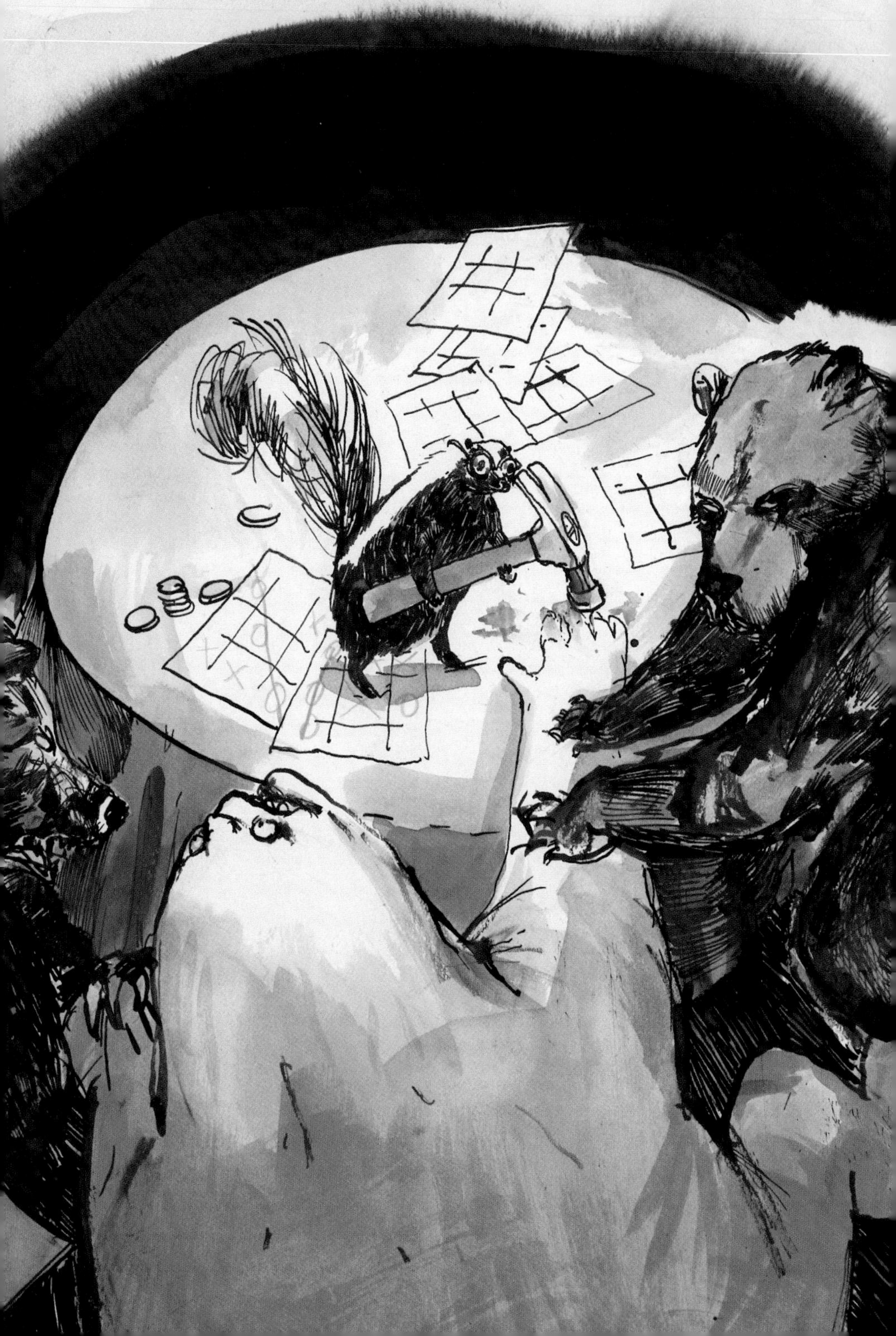

Bigfoot sometime get called
rolling stone.
Called irresponsible.
Have bad debt.
Trail of bad lady relationship.
No can help.

I a hunter -
gatherer.

And maybe just a bit
of an asshole.

Comeback

Bigfoot mention before that things going bad in career lately. Got dumped by agent last week and bank foreclose on summer hut in woods. I down but not out yet. All sort of plan in works. Frankly, this book big part of it. Think of call it 'No More Bigfoot Lie, Bitchez'. Think title good and hip-hop edgy. Editor not think it go over so good in middle America. Also hurt chances of get in Oprah Book Club. After I crush editor skull with fax machine, realize maybe he right. Thankfully he pull through.

Manage retain 67% brain function.

You *go* girl!

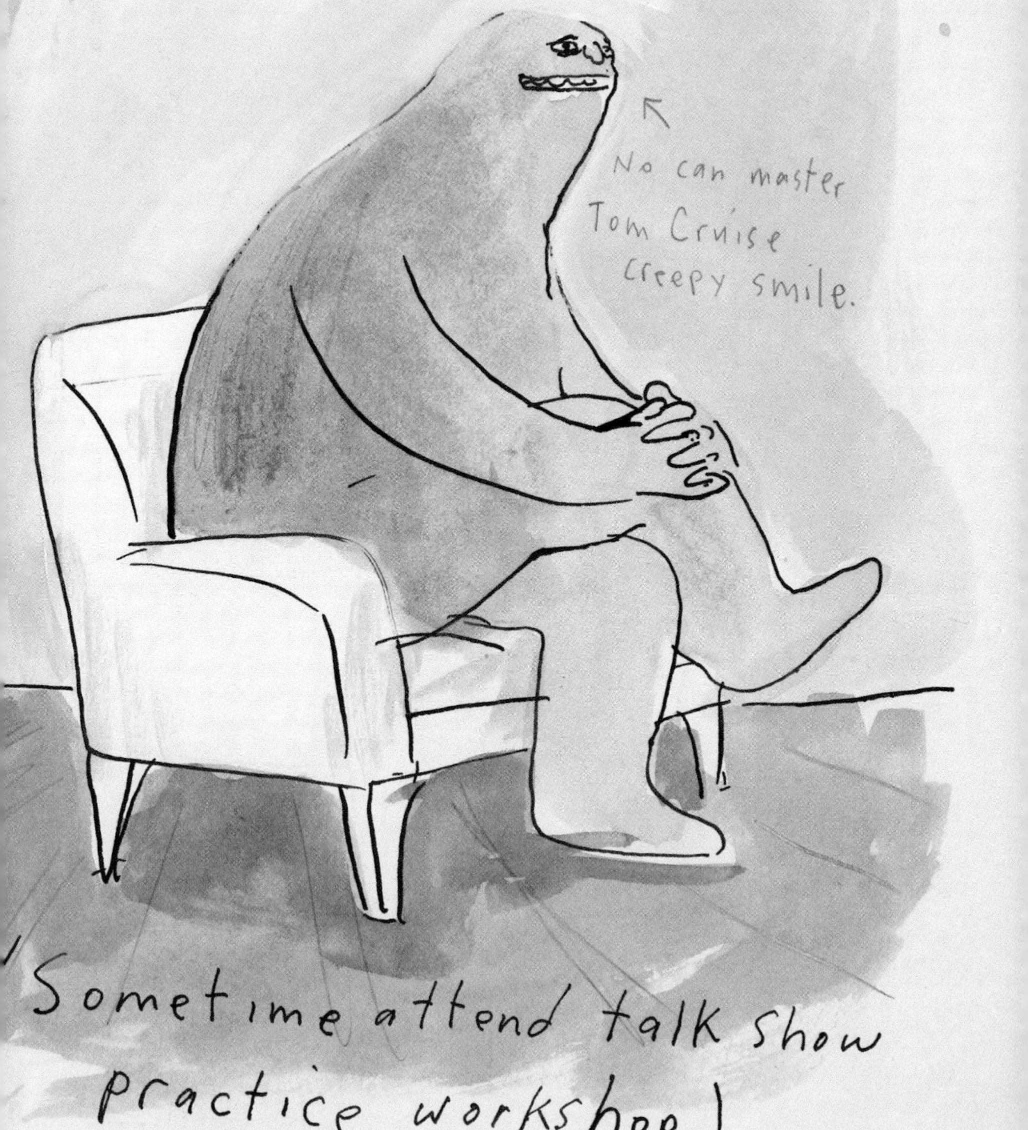

No can master Tom Cruise creepy smile.

(Sometime attend talk show practice workshop.)

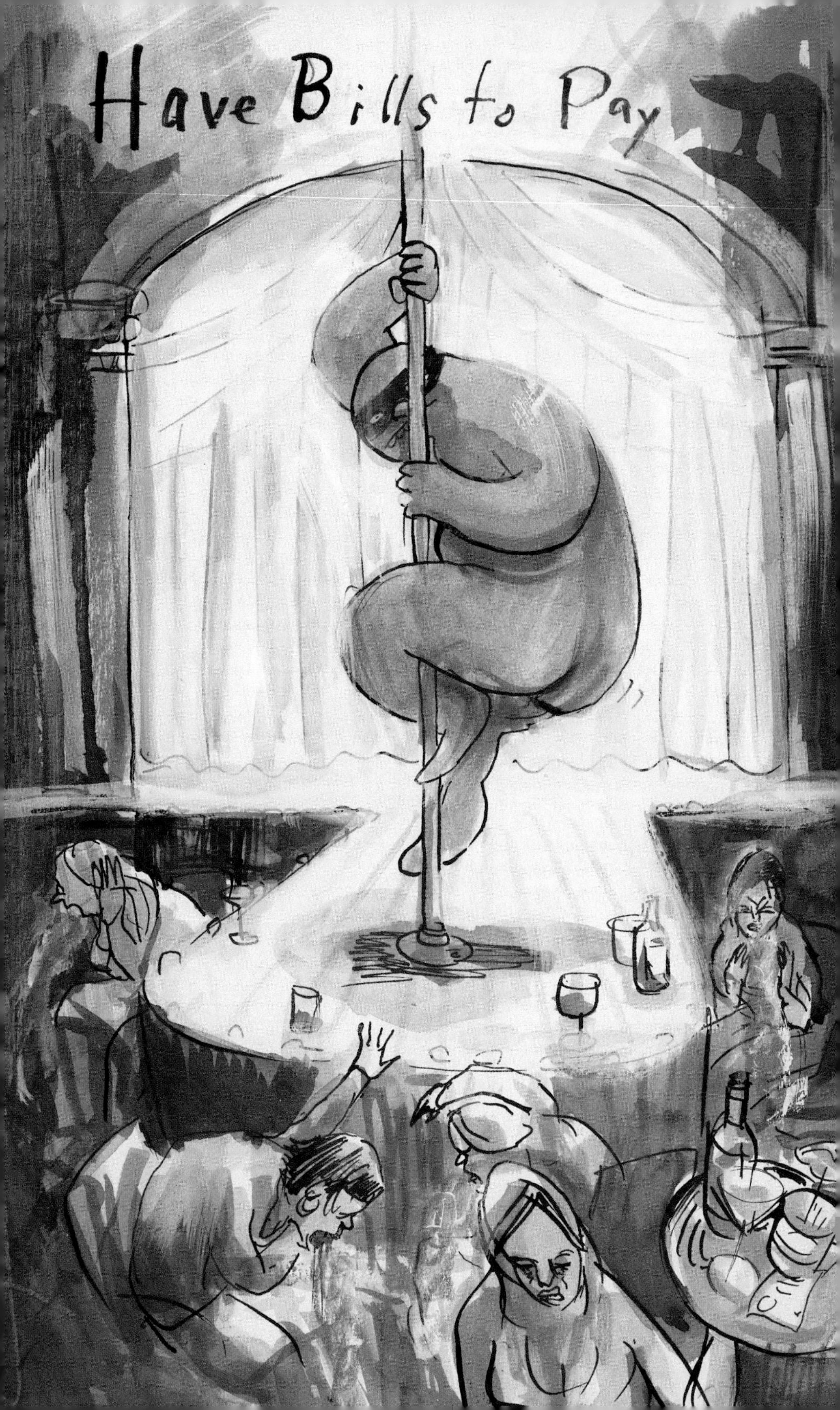
Have Bills to Pay

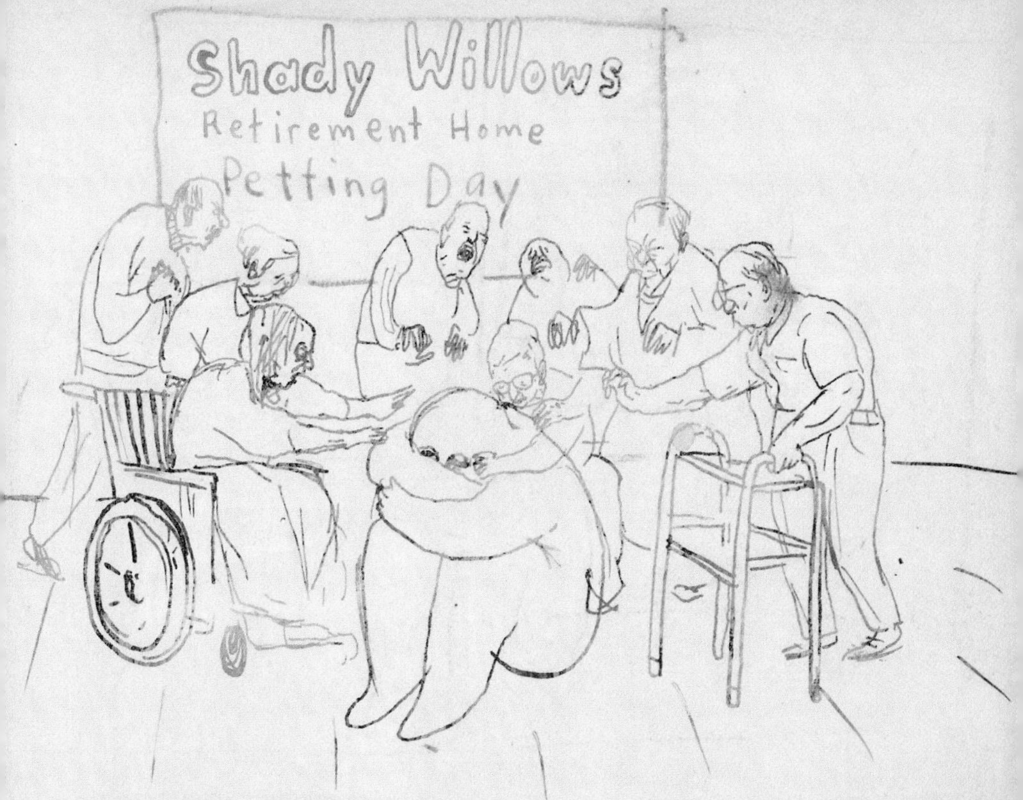

Shady Willows
Retirement Home
Petting Day

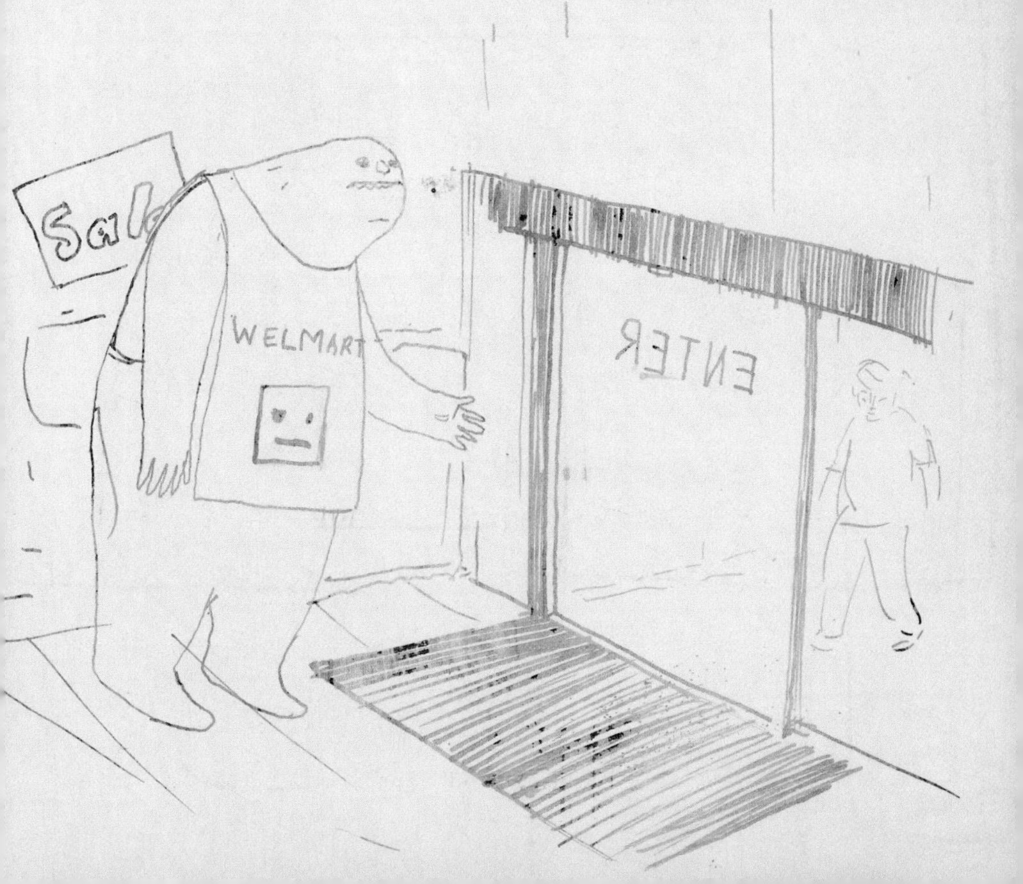

WELMART
ENTER

Natural

Computer generated movie
monster can kiss Bigfoot ass.
No have range like Bigfoot.

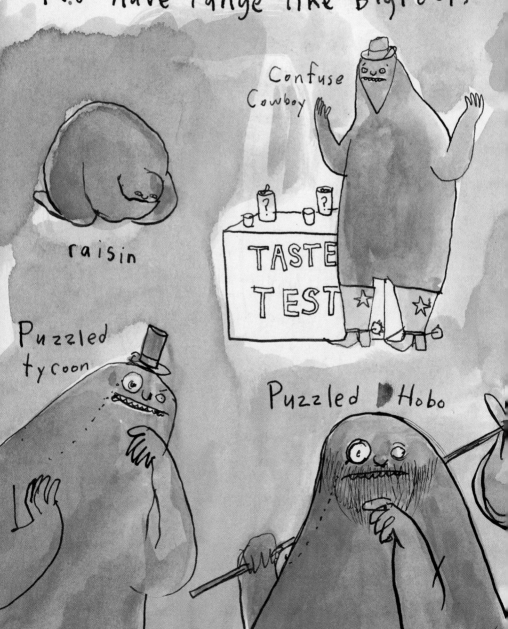

Confuse
Cowboy

raisin

TASTE
TEST

Puzzled
tycoon

Puzzled Hobo

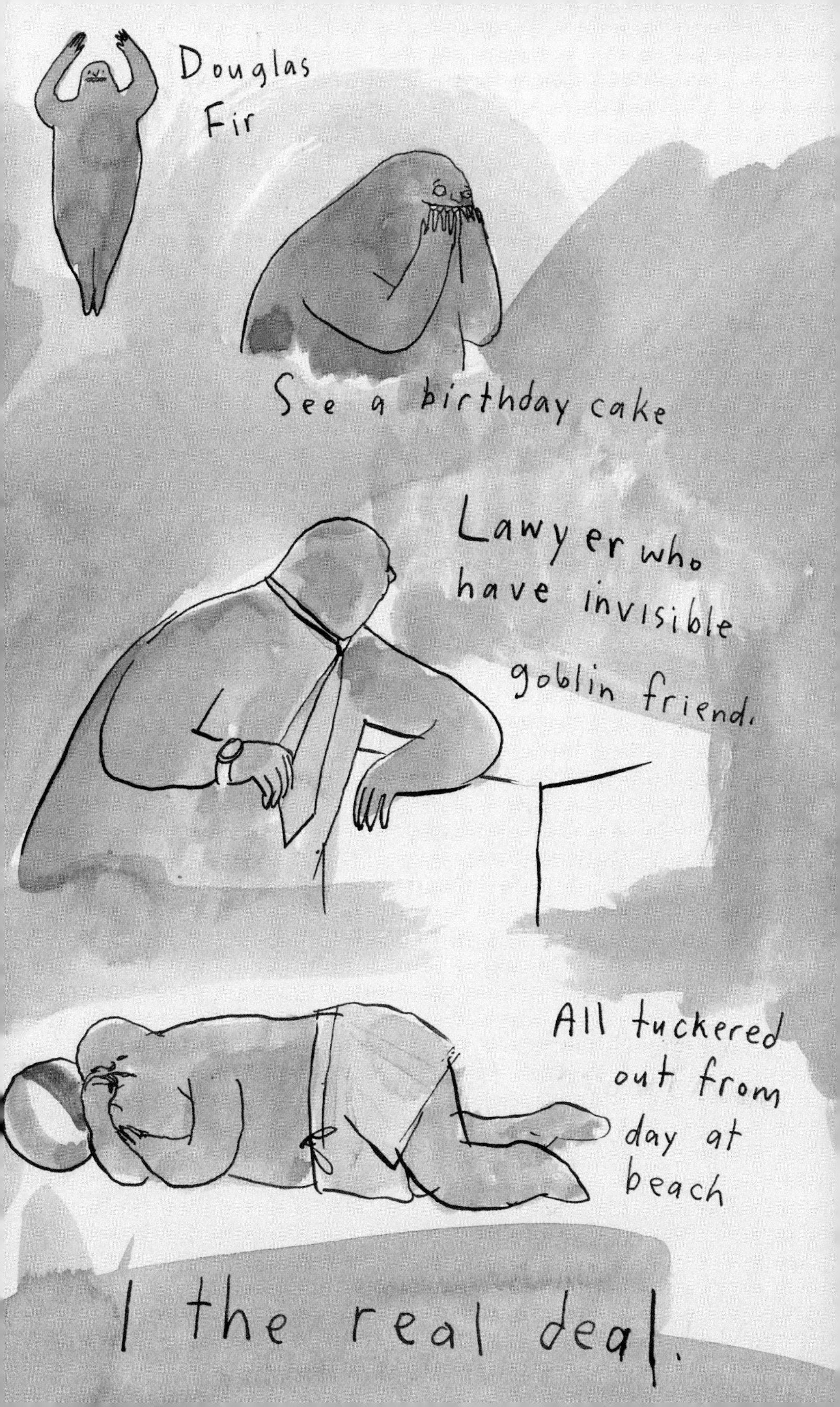
Douglas Fir
See a birthday cake
Lawyer who have invisible goblin friend.
All tuckered out from day at beach
I the real deal.

Undermine

Spend life trying build cool image.
Try be serious, try be frightening.
Still people laugh at Bigfoot.
Certain element of woodland
society want keep Bigfoot down.
They run slander campaign.

Try eat them but they run up
tree.

Cunning.

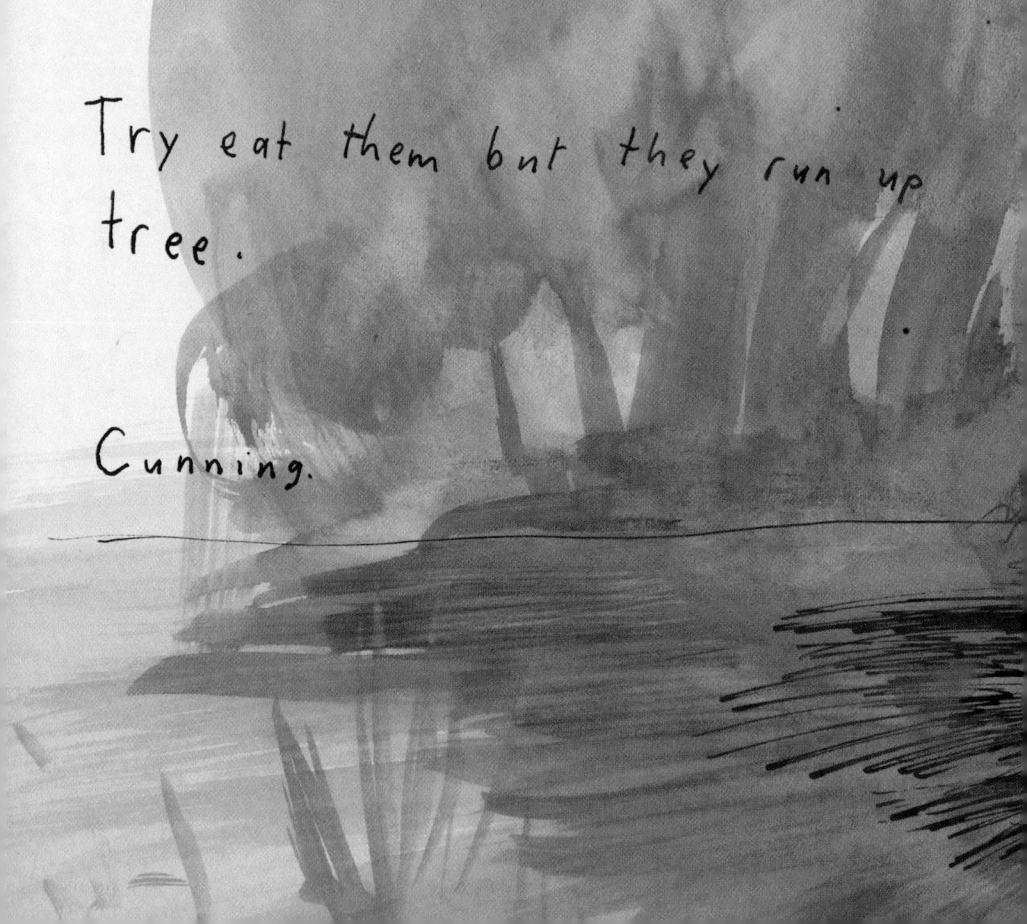

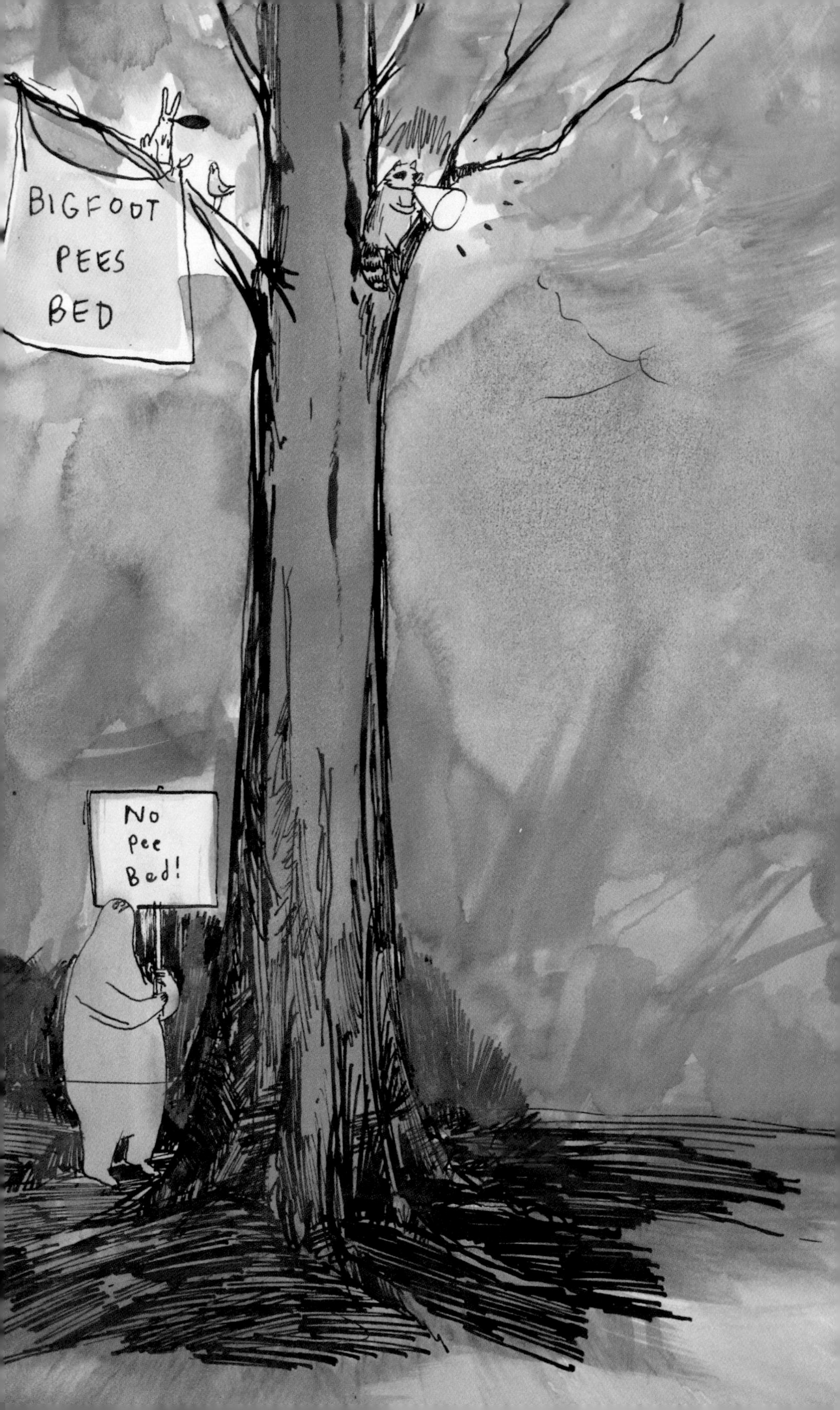
BIGFOOT PEES BED
No pee Bed!

Smart

Please no talk to Bigfoot like he stupid. Please no make fun of way me talk niether. Spend whole life trying to fit in but always some jerk make issue of Bigfoot lack of eloquence.

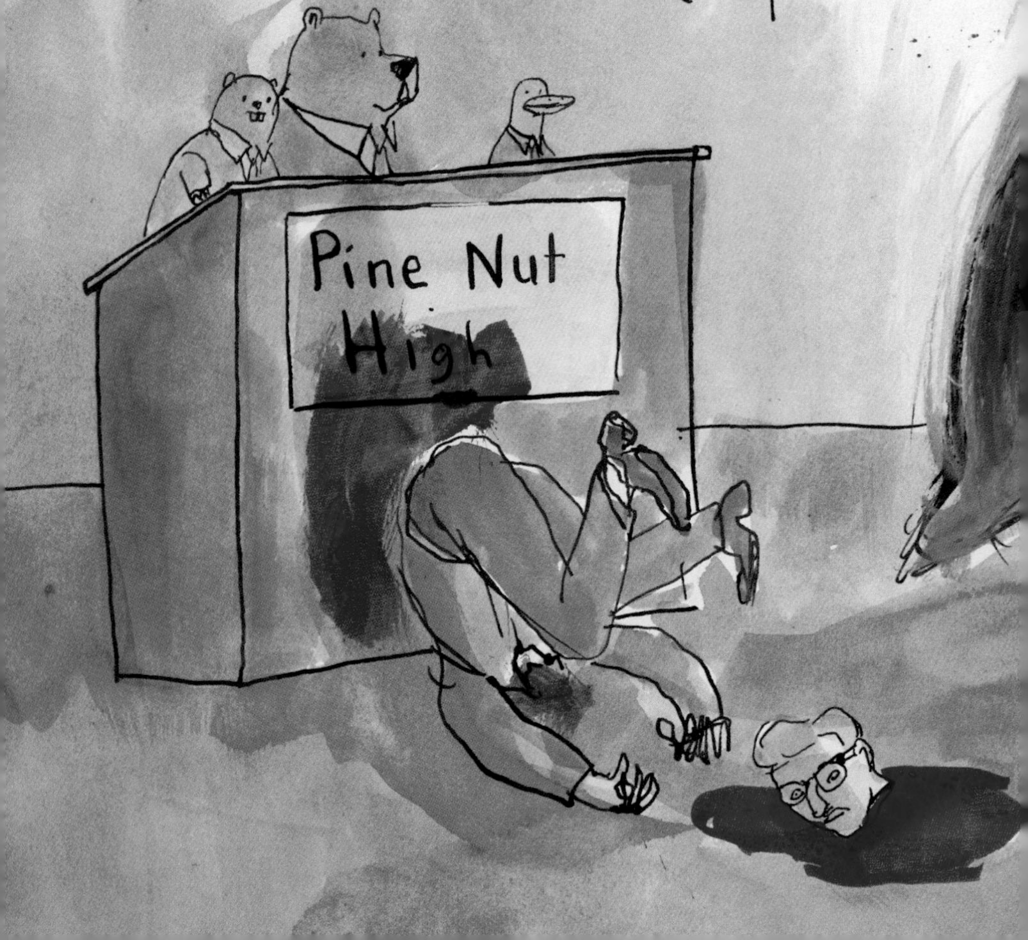
Pine Nut
High

In highschool I on debate team. Pretty good. Win lots. Smart enough to use physical advantage. That real smart, not book smart.

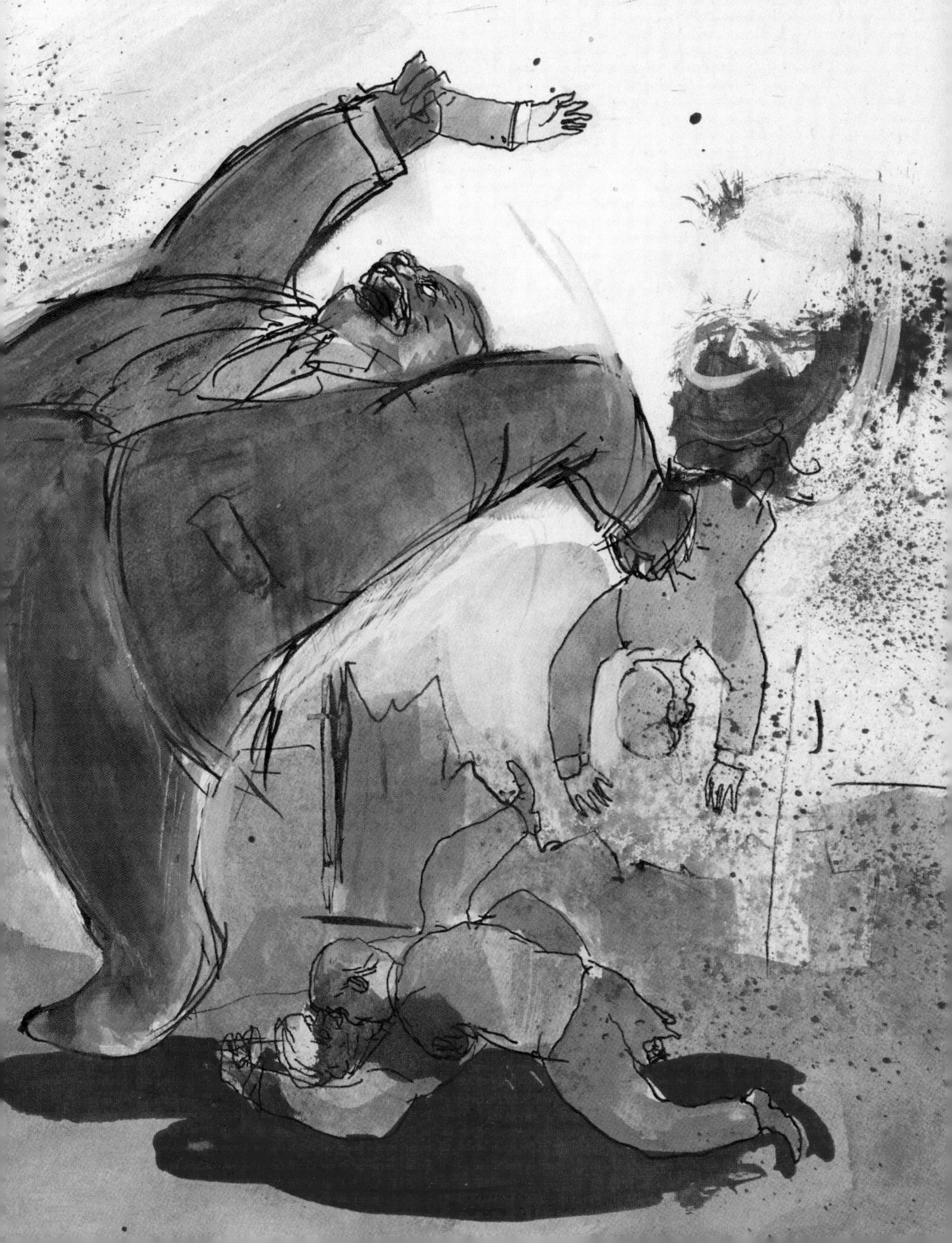

Prodigal

Bigfoot have marginalized youth
I the little Bigfoot nobody wanted
but when return from abroad all
grow up and famous I hailed
as hero.

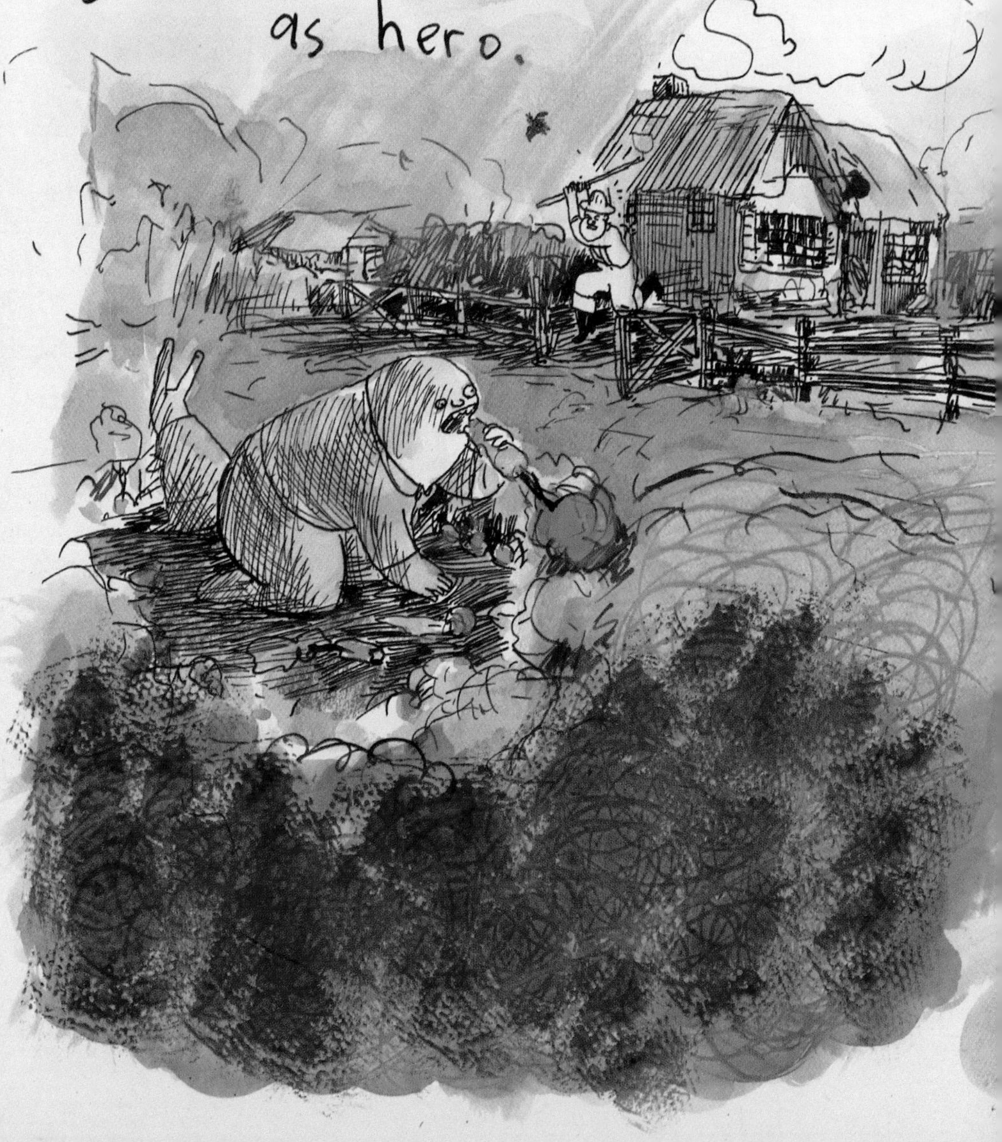

Get ticker tape parade and maked mayor.

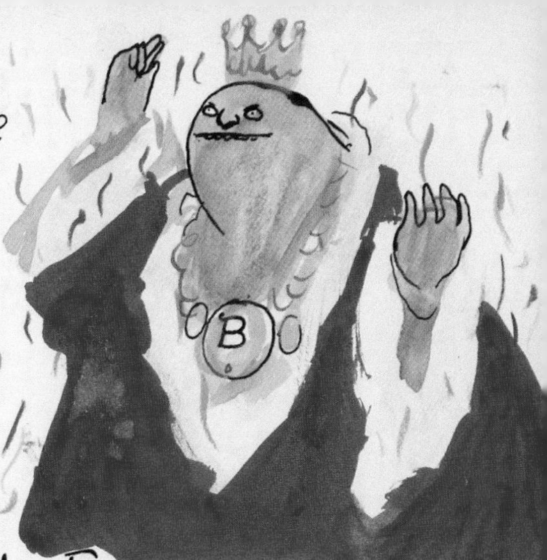
B

Now can raid Farmer Wilson carrot patch anytime want. Had him shot.

carrot never taste sweeter

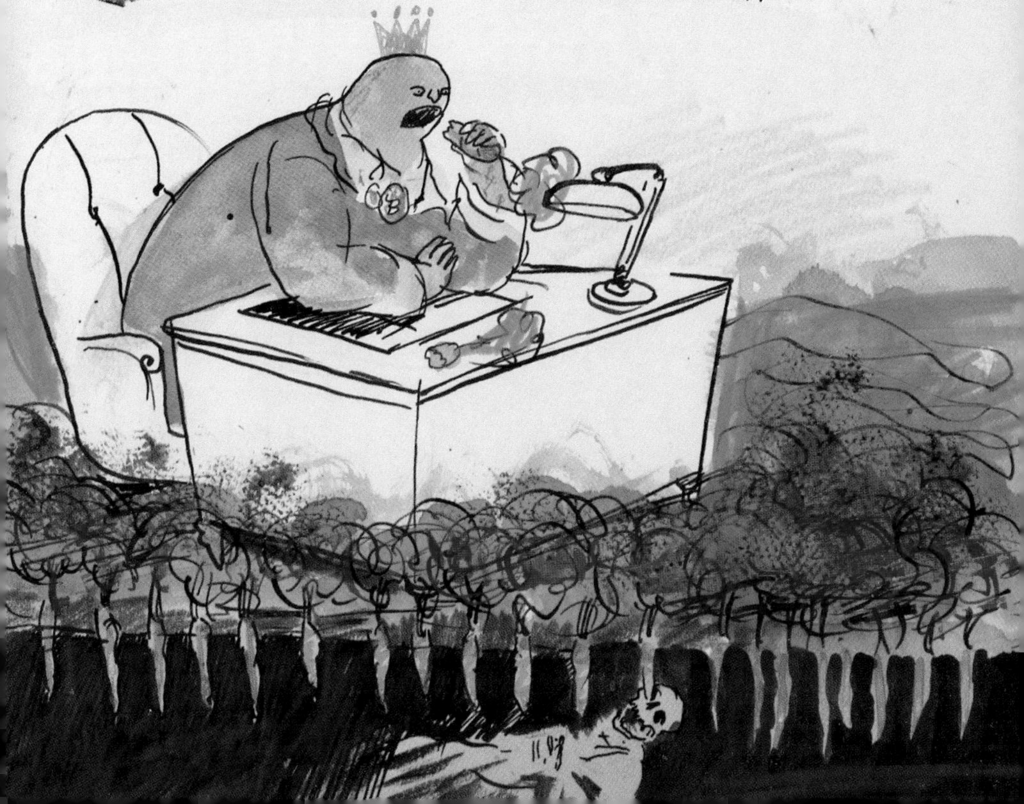

Inside

When Bigfoot go jail form gang for protection. Get respect from Chicanos, Russians, Asian triad, the Brothers, the skinhead. We have daily puppet show called "Everybody Love Raymond!"

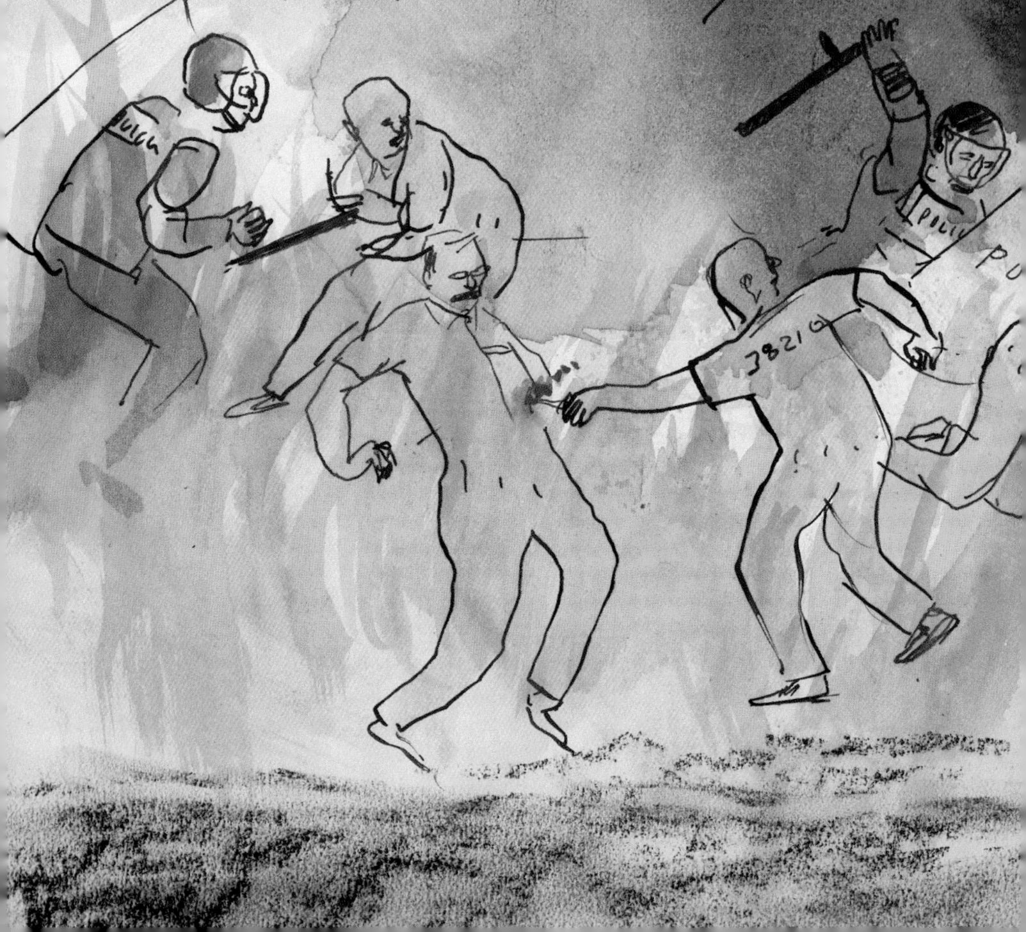
38210

Nothing like T.V. Show at all but have to cancel because of copyright violation. Also, just inappropriate title for show that take place in prison. "...terribly misleading." write one reviewer.

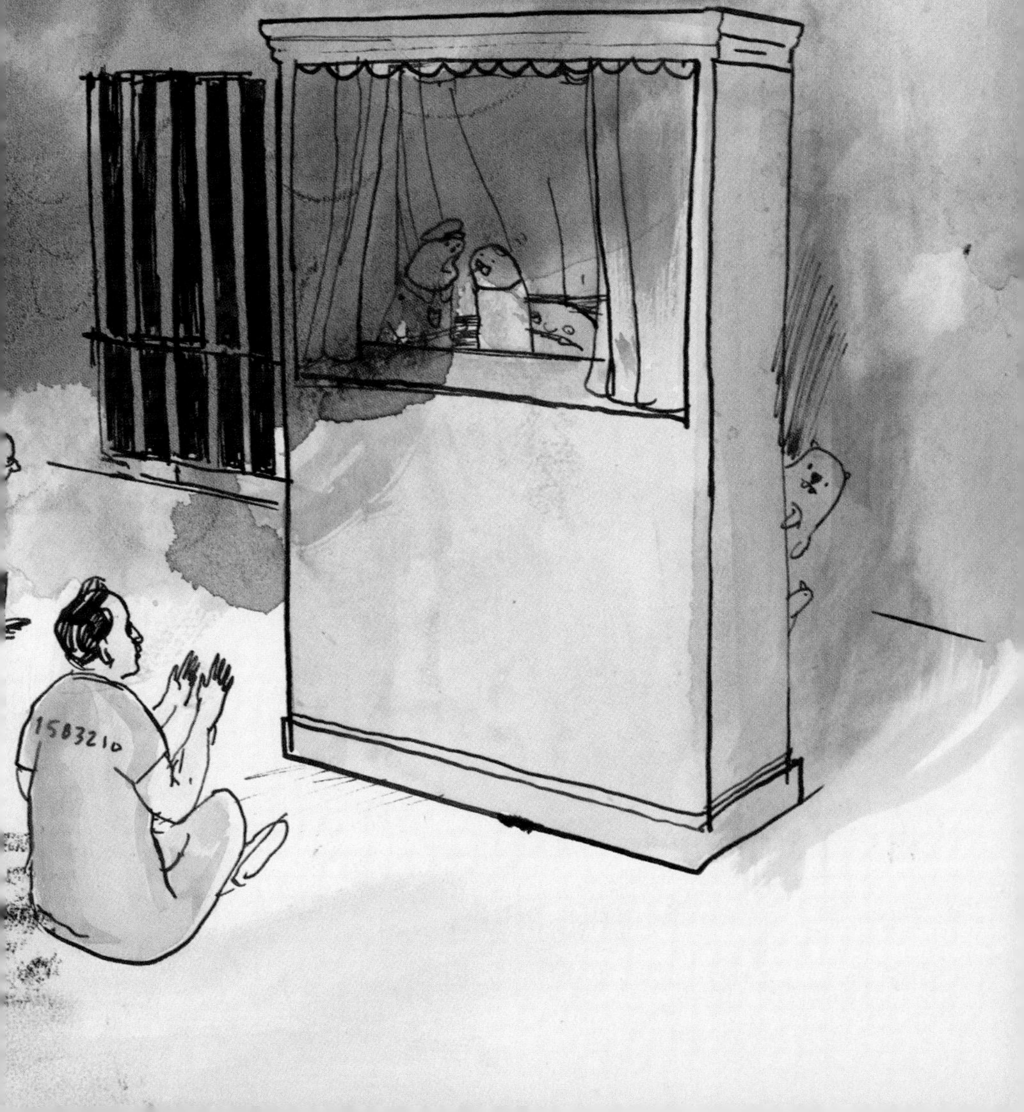
1503210

Rare

Ok. So me. not want get up on pedistal and act all high falootin' but Bigfoot must admit I pretty special. Special-precious, not small bus special. I on a lot of lists, VIP list, christmas list, best dressed list, hit list, but me very proud of being on endangered species list because of all privalege of being in exclusive club. Some day I just pick up phone, call Black Rhino and shoot the shit. I can even use word rhino and shoot in same sentence and nobody think twice. Crazy! I get away with murder cause everyone think I fragile since I last of kind and so on. Funny part is me not sure if there is or ever was other Bigfoot. One bad thing about it though that I attract lots poachers. Apparently me gal bladder give Chinese people boners. Funny cause Chinese people give me boner too but Bigfoot digress. One time poacher try to get Bigfoot organs. He expert Safari hunter and spend weeks stalking me and learning Bigfoot ways. He see my love for Count Chocula and hide in fridge disguise as giant milk carton. Day before he want poach Bigfoot decide go low carb. diet so no Chocula. Man freeze to death in fridge. Bigfoot also have cirrhosis at time so it convenient for me use him for liver transplant donor. Bigfoot enjoy irony.

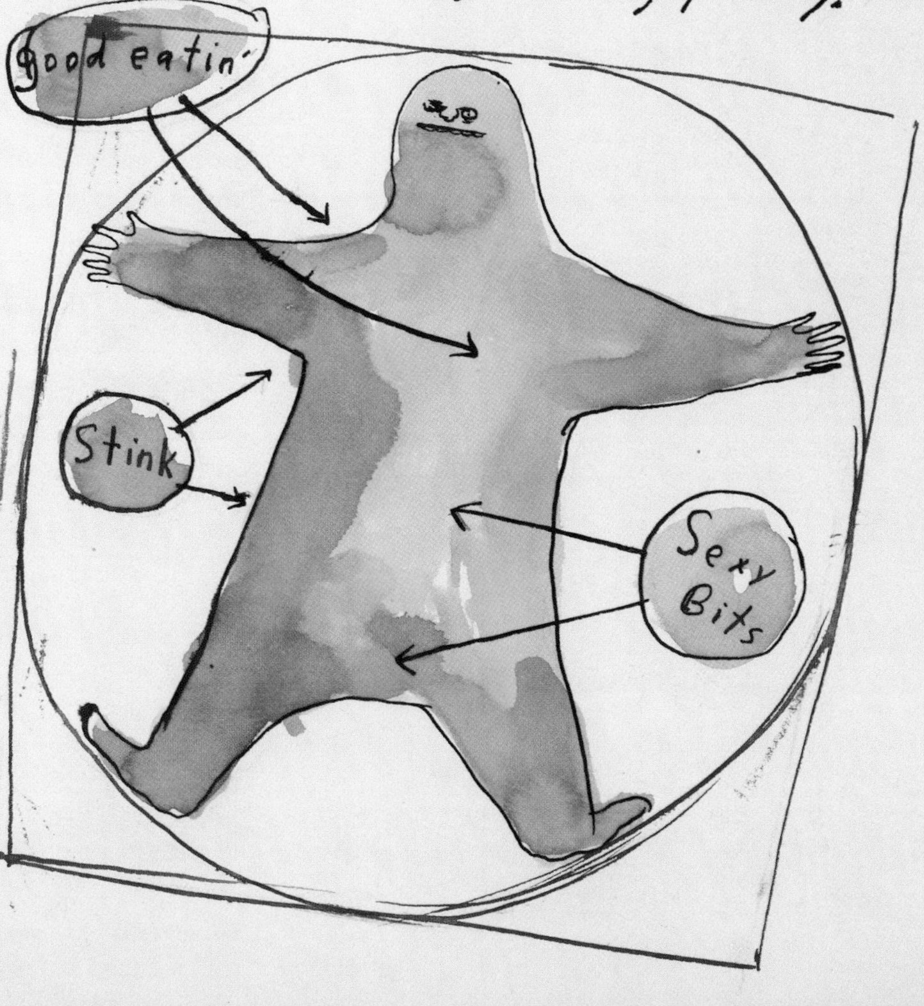
good eatin'
Stink
Sexy Bits

Daddy?

Though I not know who you are I thin
I see you one day in window of passing
bus. I chase after and yell and cry unti
lung burst and Bigfoot
collapse by side of road.

Daddy, where you be?
Have so many question.
Have so much to share.

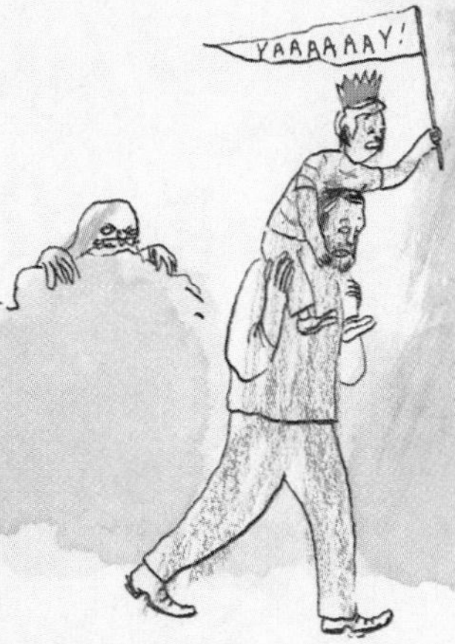
YAAAAAAY!

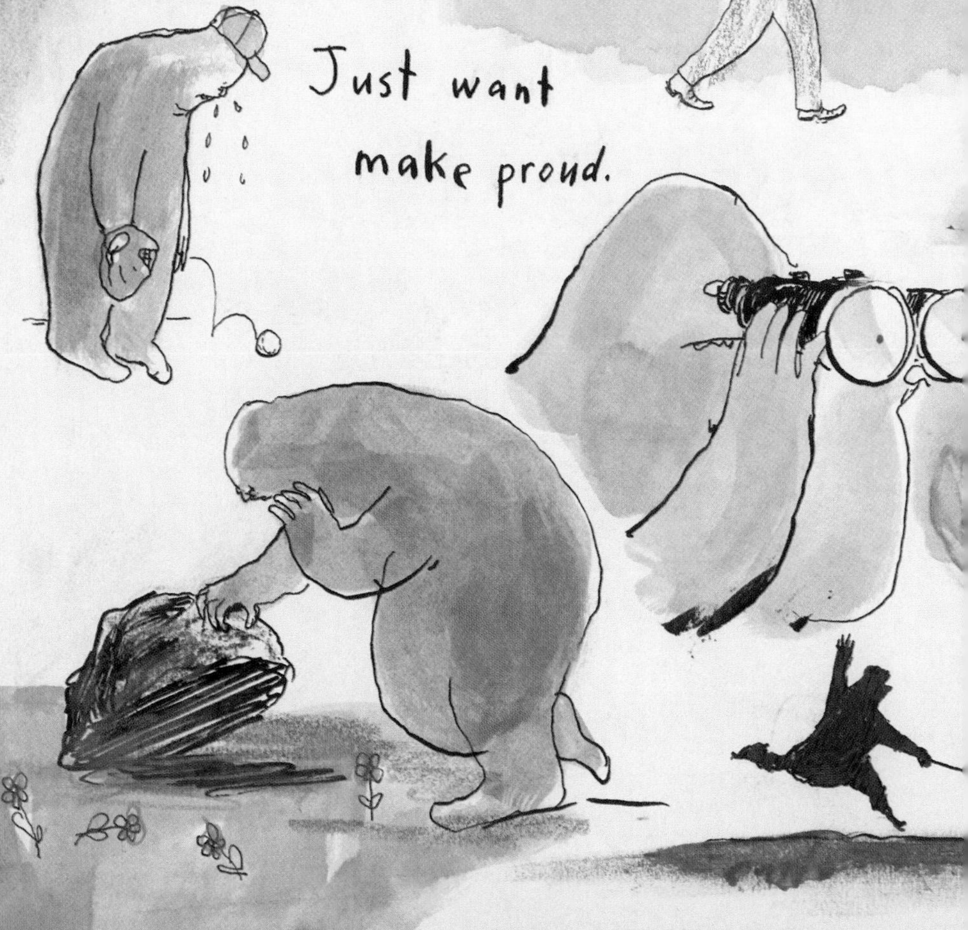

Just want
make proud.

ne time at school get in debate with
ommy. He say he Dad beat up me Dad.
Say "No!", he say "Yes!". I Know not what
lse do so I slam Tommy head against
desk until he stop live.
ther time I chase ducks
round pond with stick
overed in poop. That
ime lung burst from laughing
so hard. Anyway, if you want
find me it pretty easy since
really big star now.

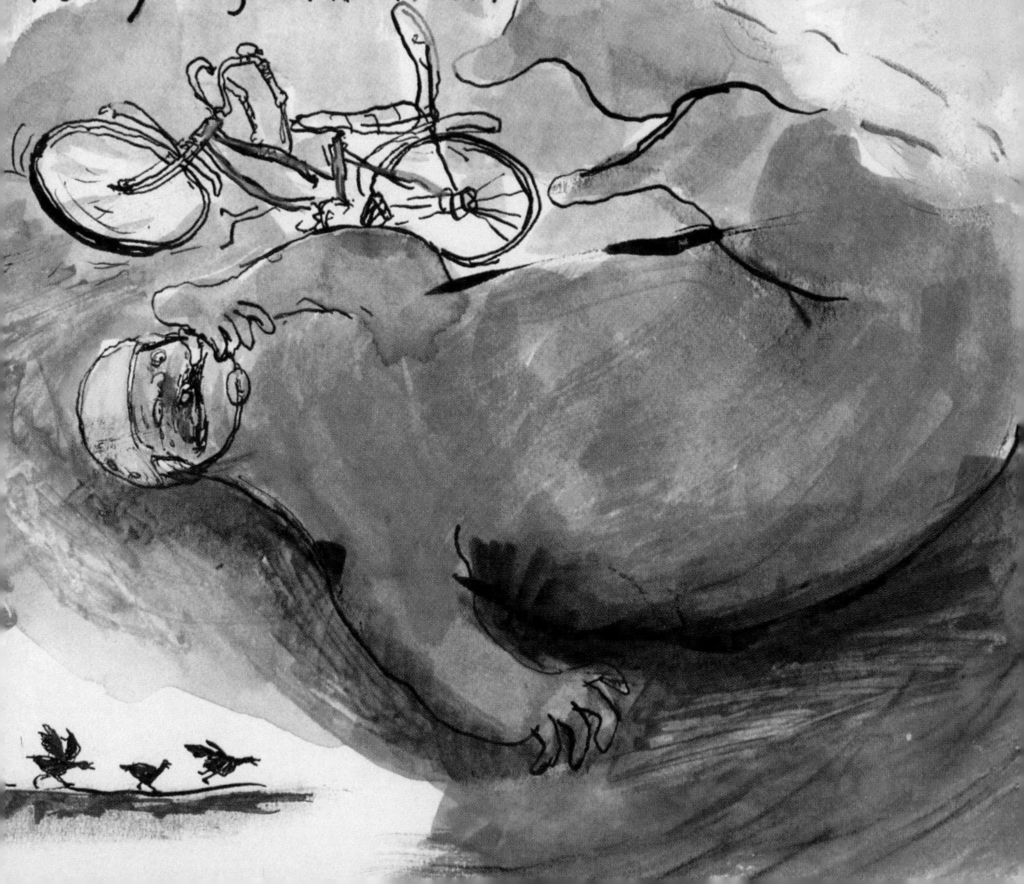

Give A Hoot

Find half a corn dog in foyer this morning. It Not first time. Hey listen! No Serious! Shut up! You people filthy and it make Bigfoot angry like Henry Rollins. Volunteer for Park Service anti-litter mascot but turned down for radical views. Either you with Bigfoot or against. Please join as I quite lonely. Have rad logo and catchy slogan. Also, free cookie and milk at meetings

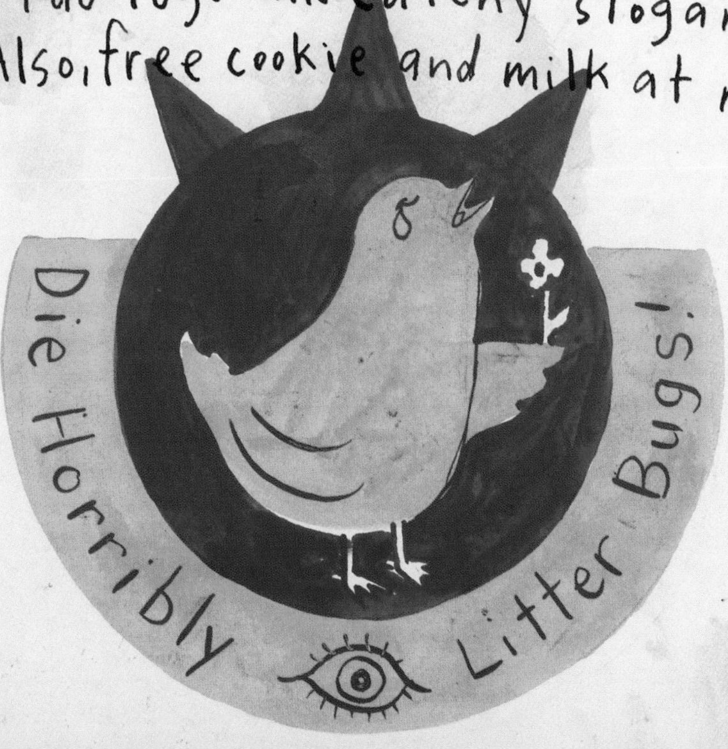
Die Horribly
Litter Bugs!

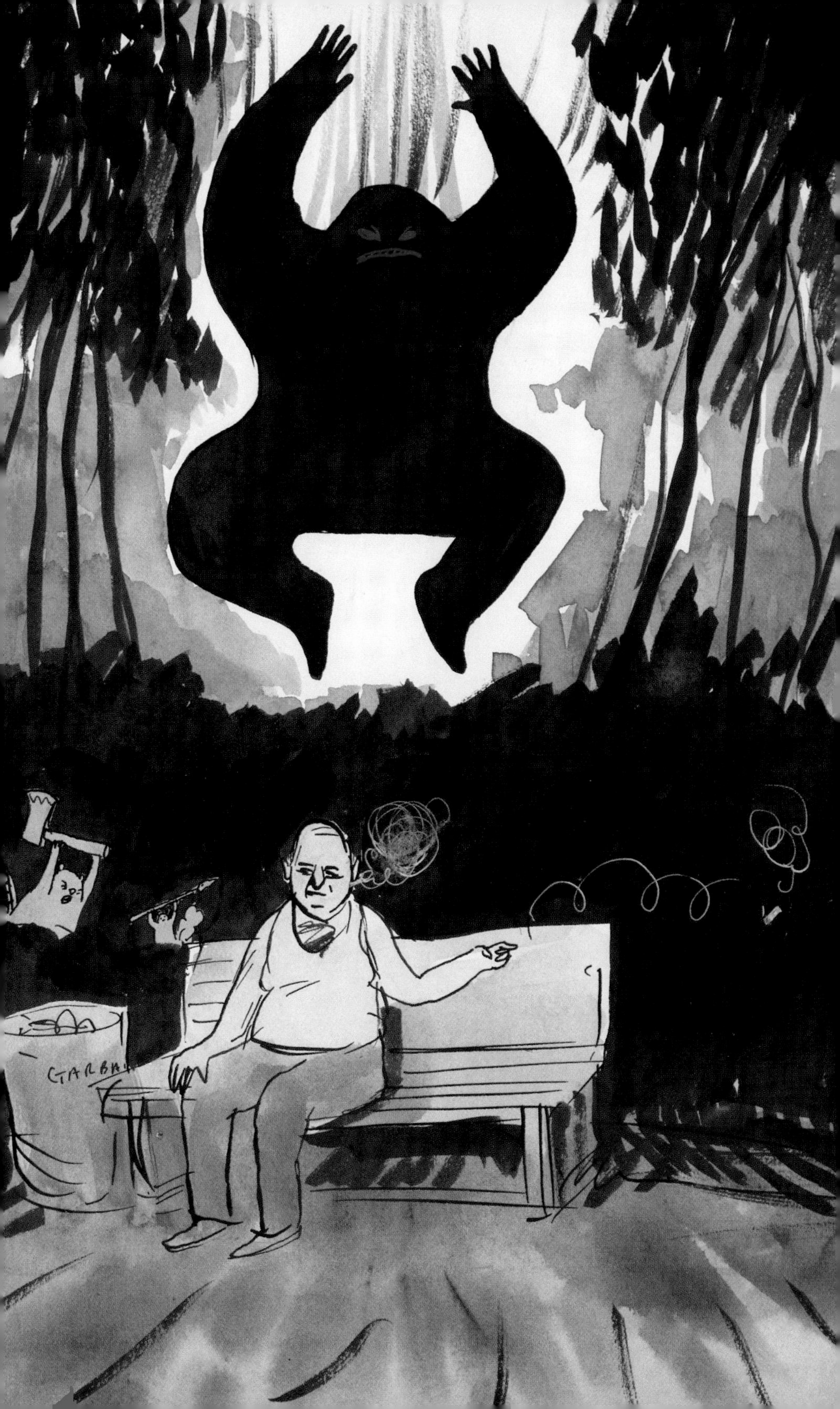
GARBA

Danger! Warren!

Warren what have I tell you? Warren! Warren are you listen? Warren it three week since you come home. WARREN JOINING A GANG NOT THE ANSWER Don't go throw you life away.

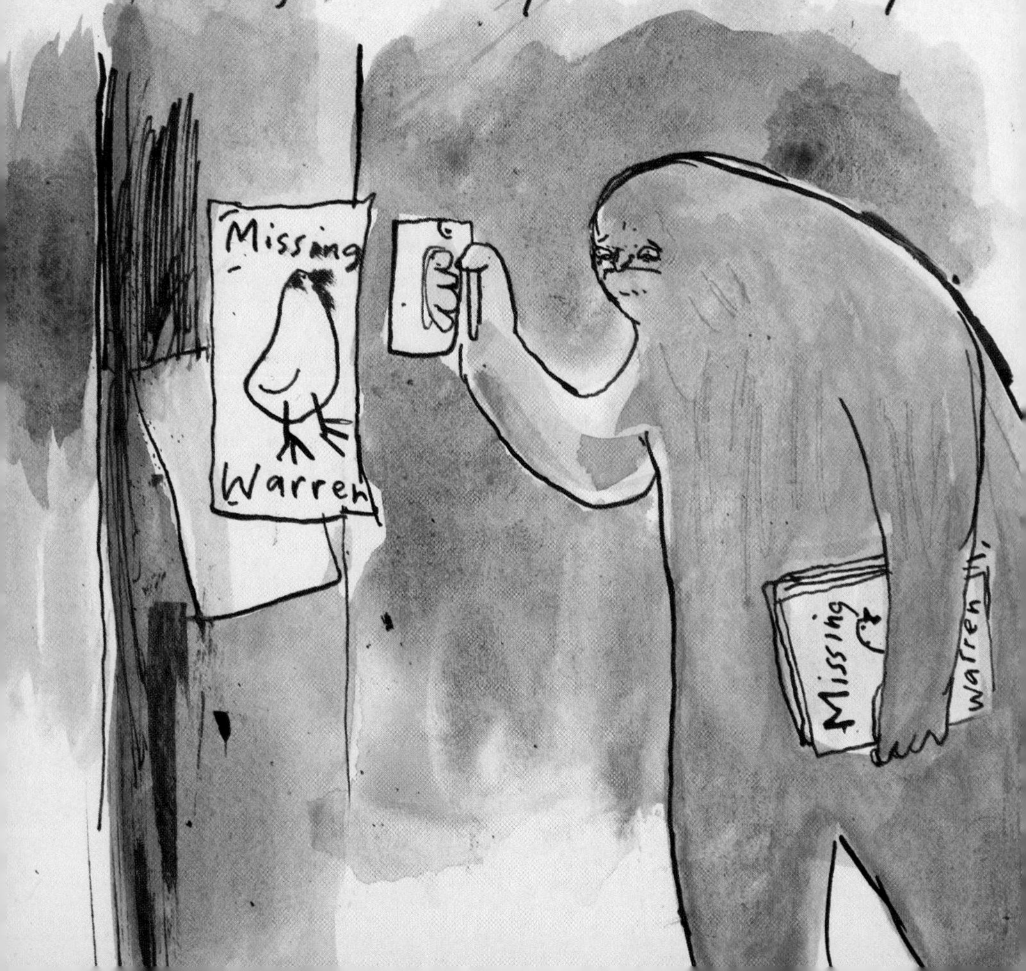

Missing
Warren
Missing
Warren

You better than this. You got the mad B-ball skillz. You play college ball no problem. Get degree in I.T., make good money. Maybe go Pro. Not take life of crime. Selling gun and drug and mackin' hoes.

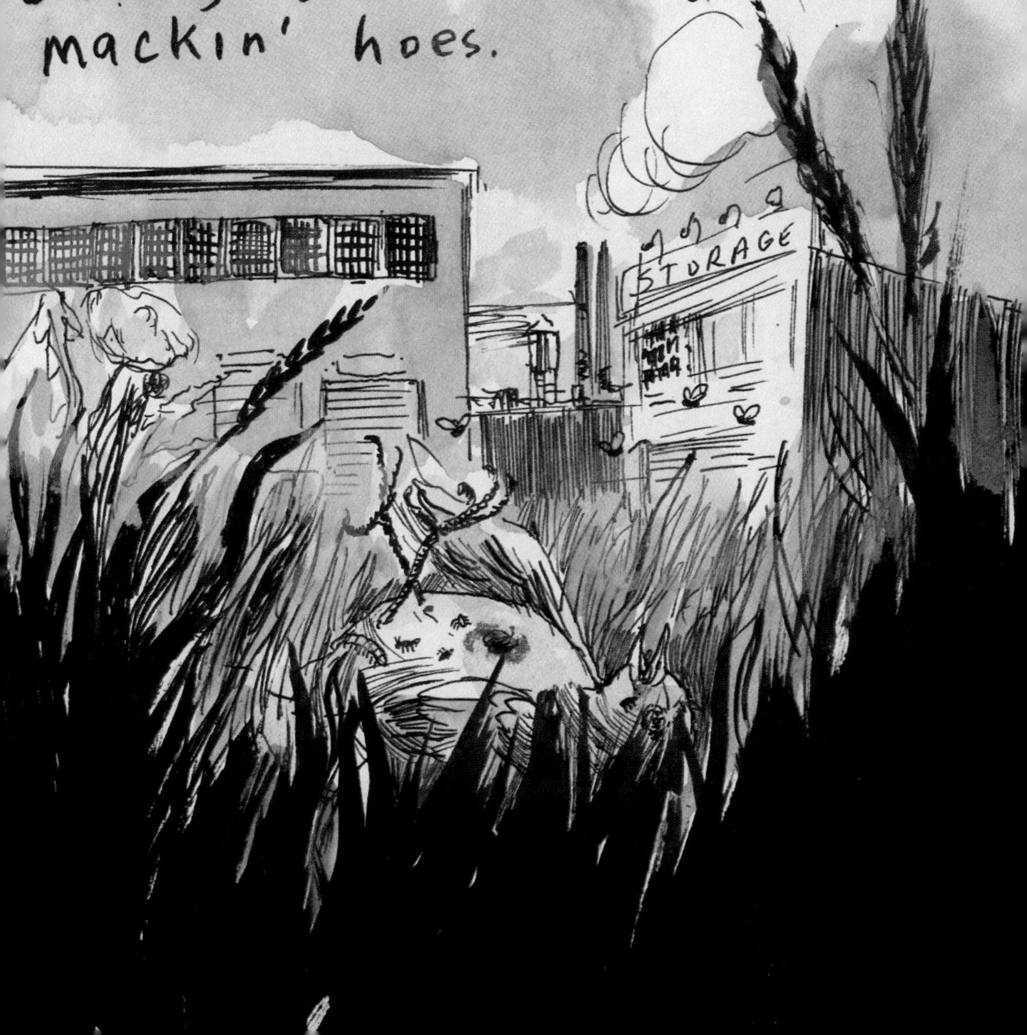
STORAGE

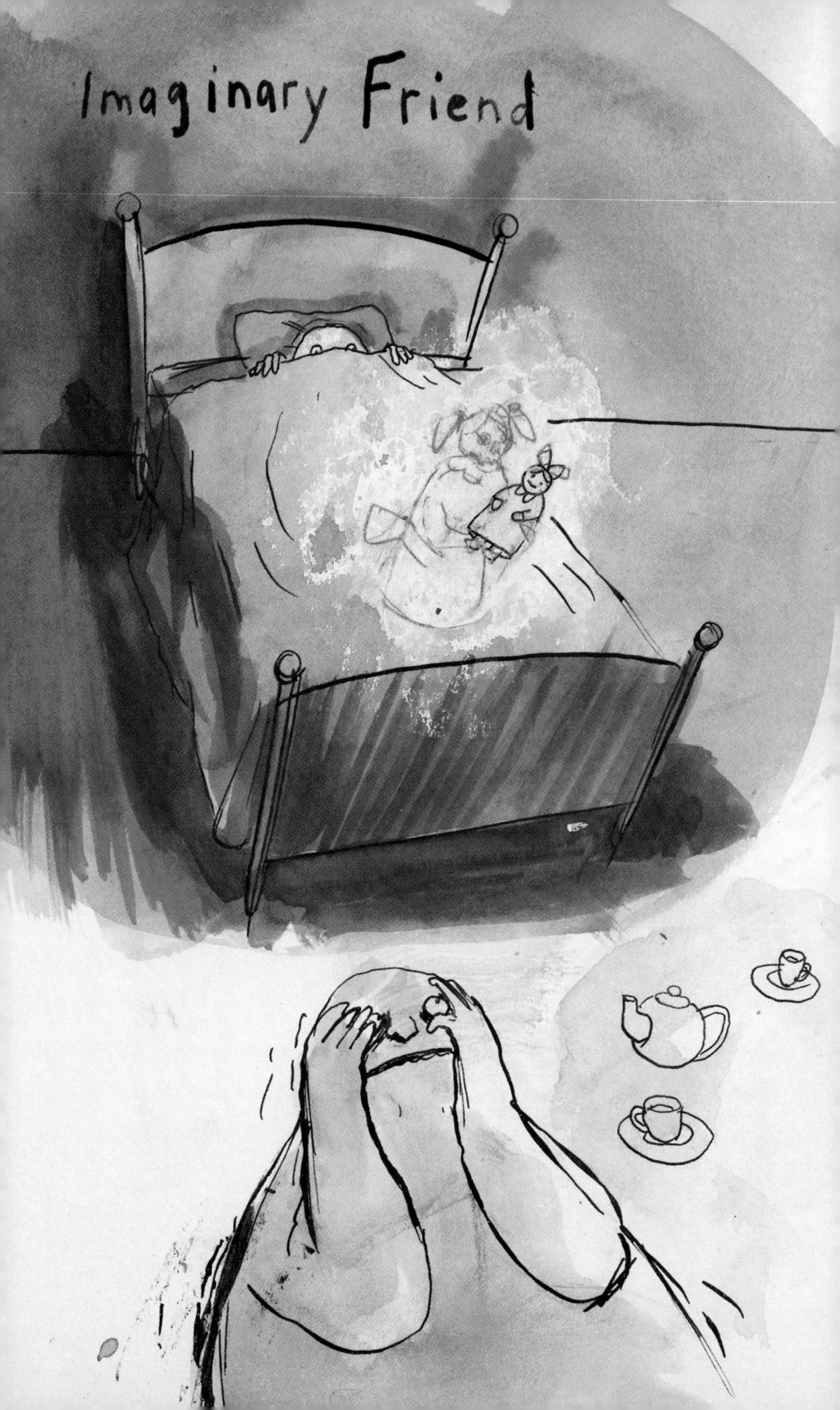
Imaginary Friend

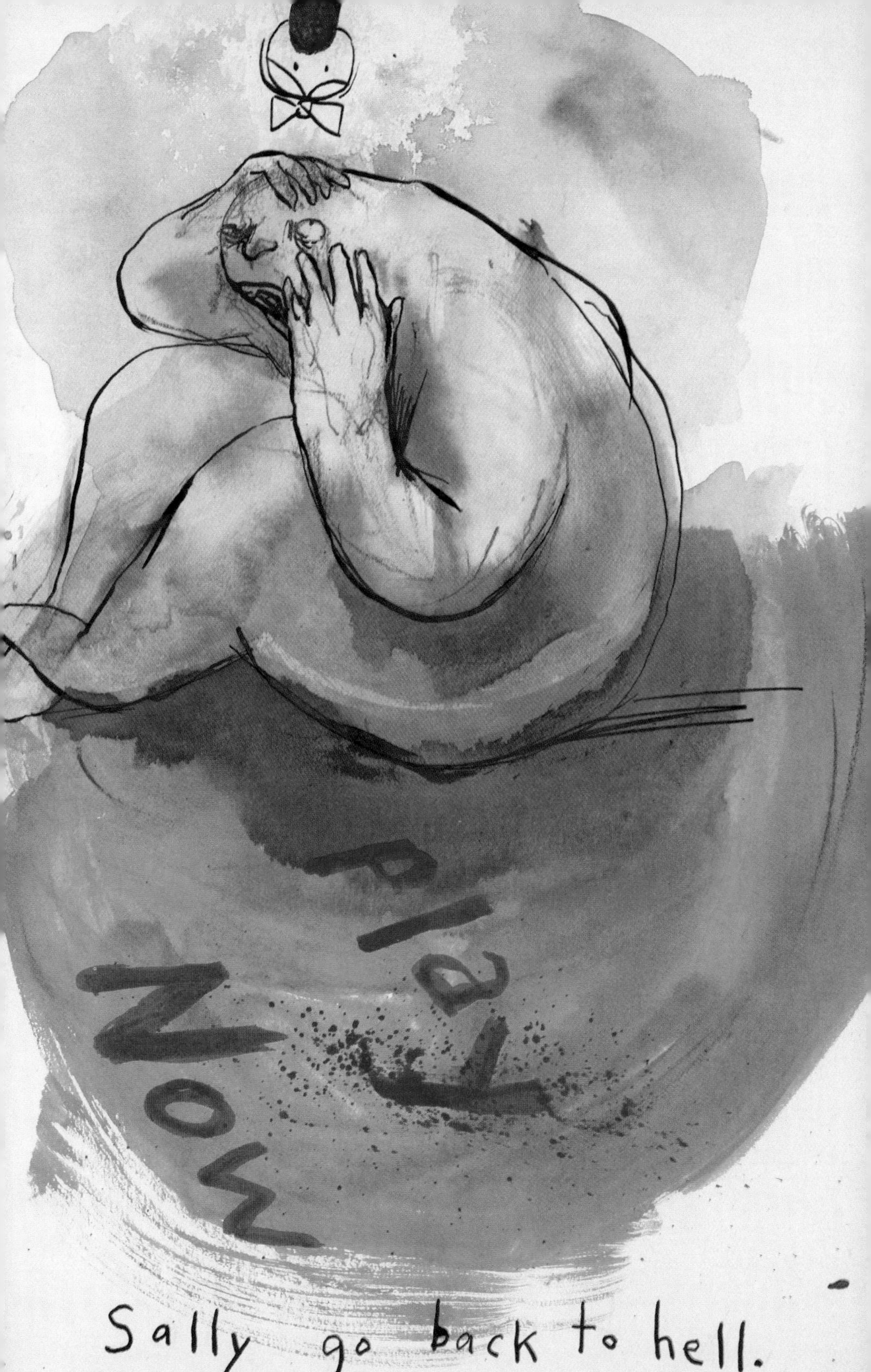
Now
play

Sally go back to hell.

Dirty Deed Done Dirt Cheap.

One time ago me have embarassing episode where Bigfoot have too much peach schnapps for breakfast and go a little loopy. So me maybe get a little naked and maybe get a little belligerent while swimming in dolphin pool at ritzy resort. Maybe I relieve self on dolphin in said pool. What big deal officer? That why pool have filter, that why pencil have eraser. Catch Bigfoot once, shame on Bigfoot, Catch Bigfoot twice, more shame on Bigfoot me guess. Whatever. So anyways big show trial happen, media have field day, I guilty before even started. John Walsh demand I get chair. Courtroom sketch artist make Bigfoot like antichrist. Such bullshit. Bigfoot convicted for indecent exposure even though Bigfoot no even normal wear clothes. Me get sentenced to community service. Bigfoot become guide dog for blind boy Darrell. We have more fun than barrel of monkeys.

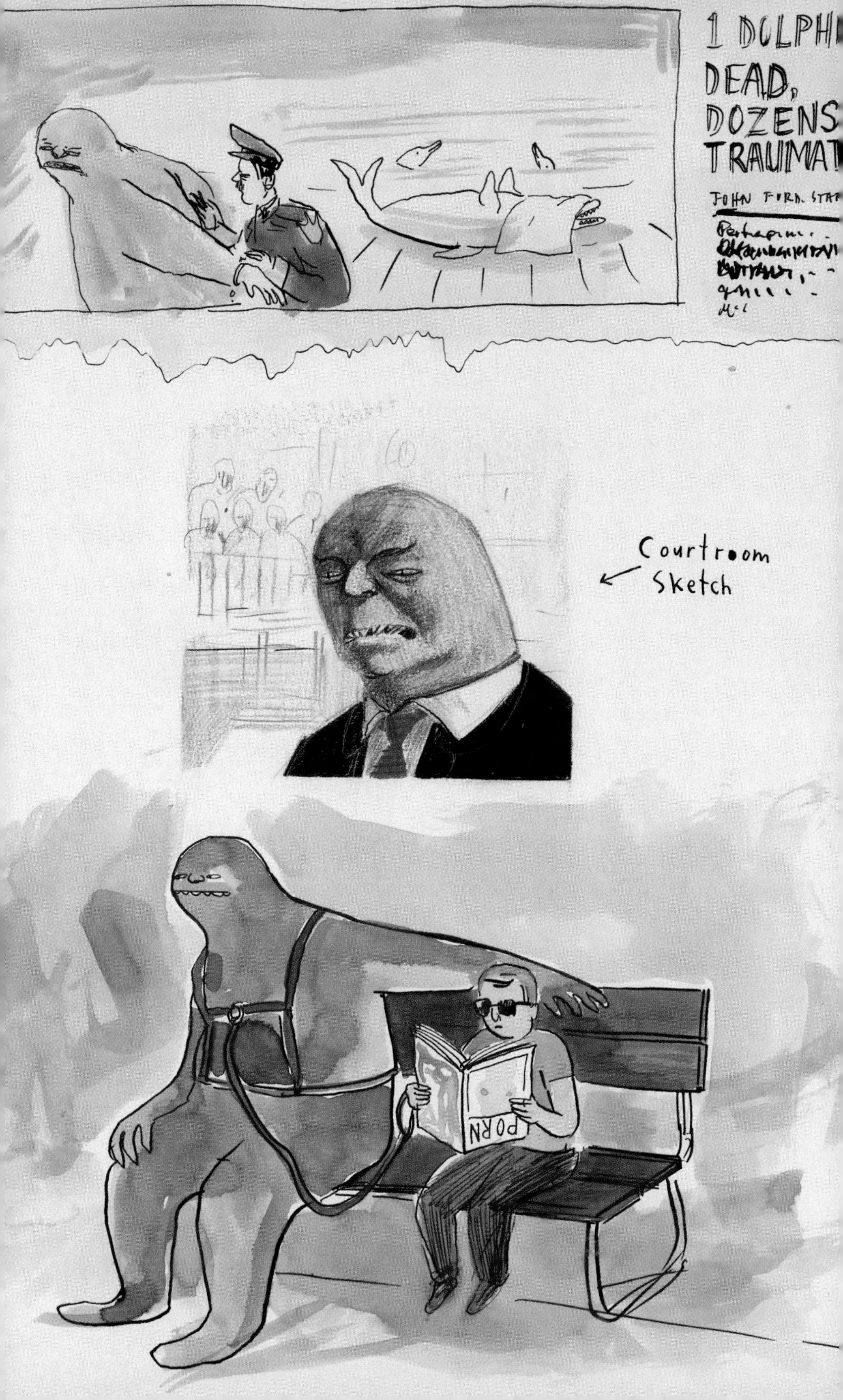
1 DOLPH
DEAD,
DOZENS
TRAUMAT
Courtroom
Sketch
PORN

You Want Come In For Drink Maybe?

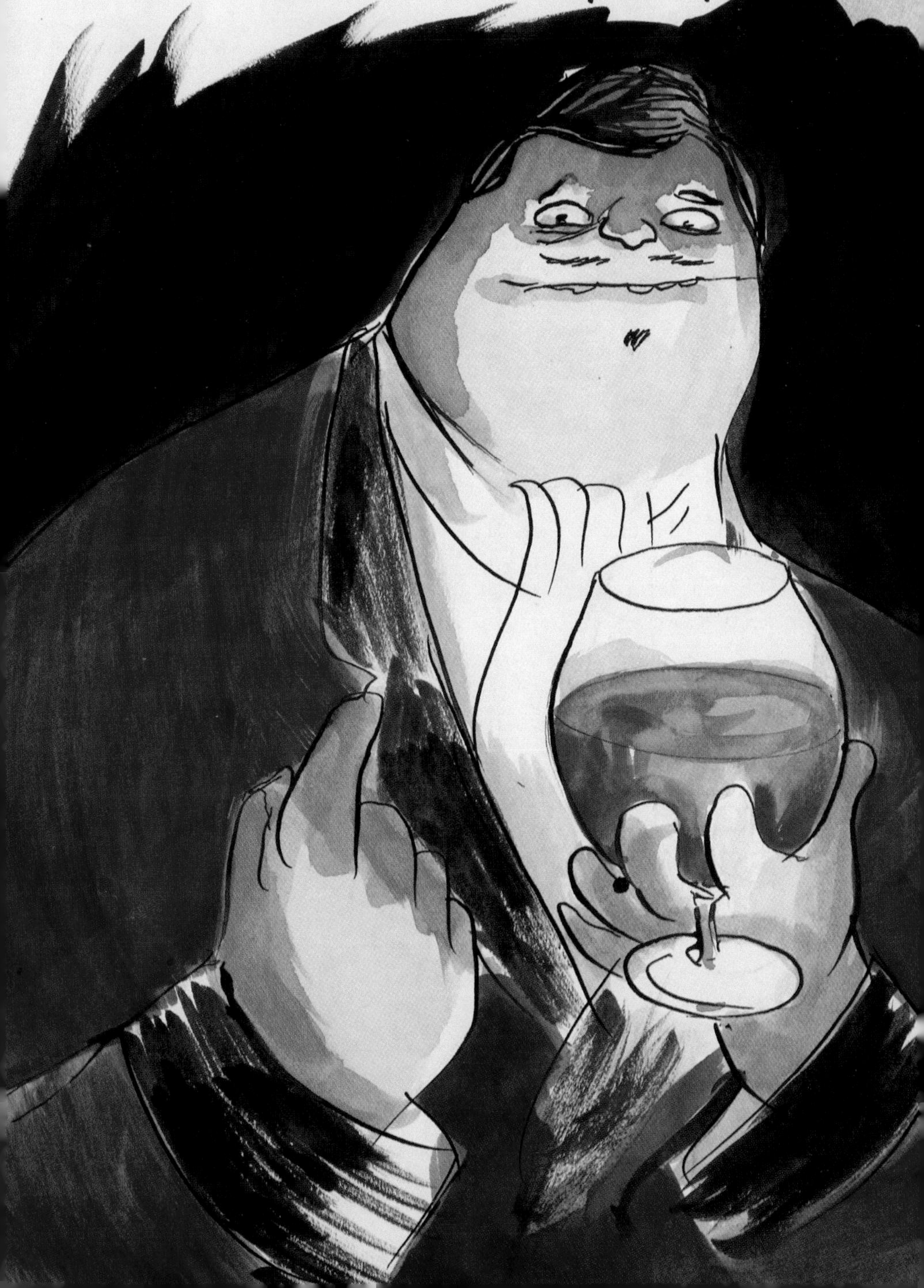

Oh no, don't worry, it no bother.
I just sitting by fire thinking how
burning ember so much like fleeting
passion of this crazy thing call life.
 So you new to neighborhood?
Let me take you coat and you
make self comfortable.
You look tense.
 Here, let Bigfoot help relax.
Bigfoot master of shoulder
massage. Mmmmm... how that?

   Let magic thumb do they
     work. You like jazz?
   I SAY YOU LIKE JAZZ?
     Hello?

   Oh, seem to have broken you
          neck.

          Canape?

Shy

Find hard talk to stranger.
Terrible at chit-chat.
Think people look at me funny
then I start panic think have to
be clever all of time.
They not understand I
artist, not entertainer?
Magic of Bigfoot what happen
when people not looking

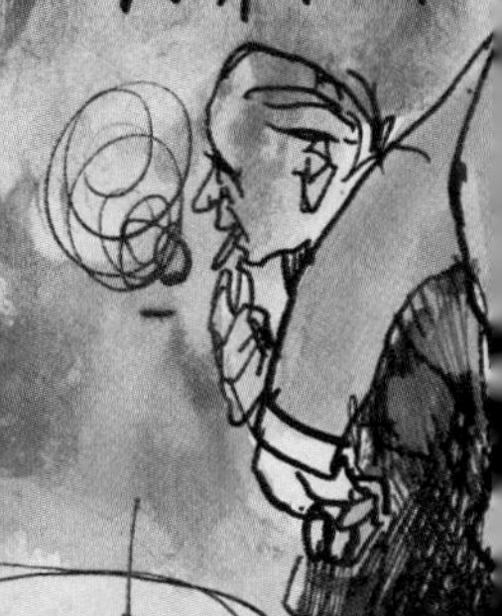

Stop looking at Bigfoot

No, please don't.

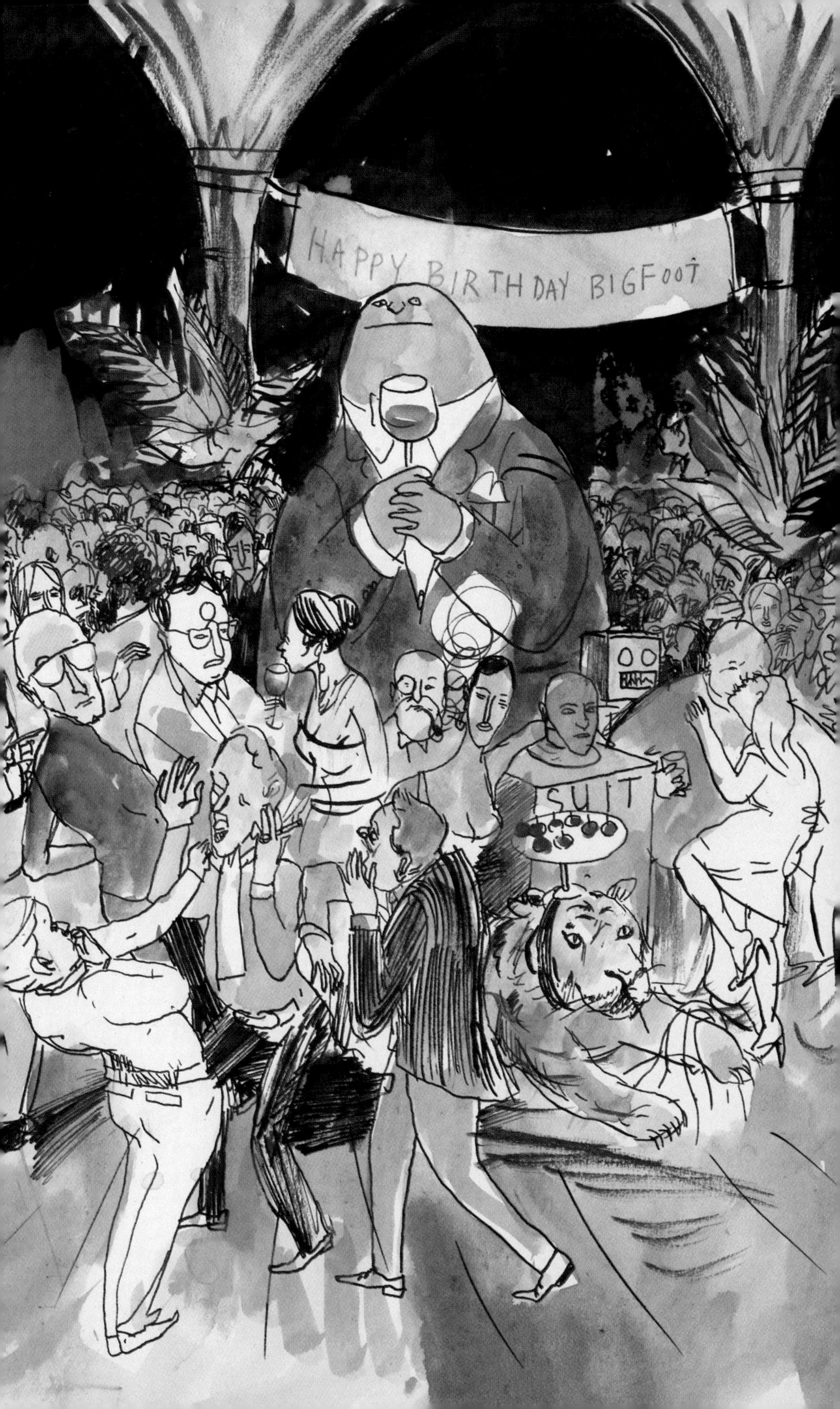
HAPPY BIRTHDAY BIGFOOT
SUIT

Deep End

Sometime me push creative envelope.

Sometime it push me.

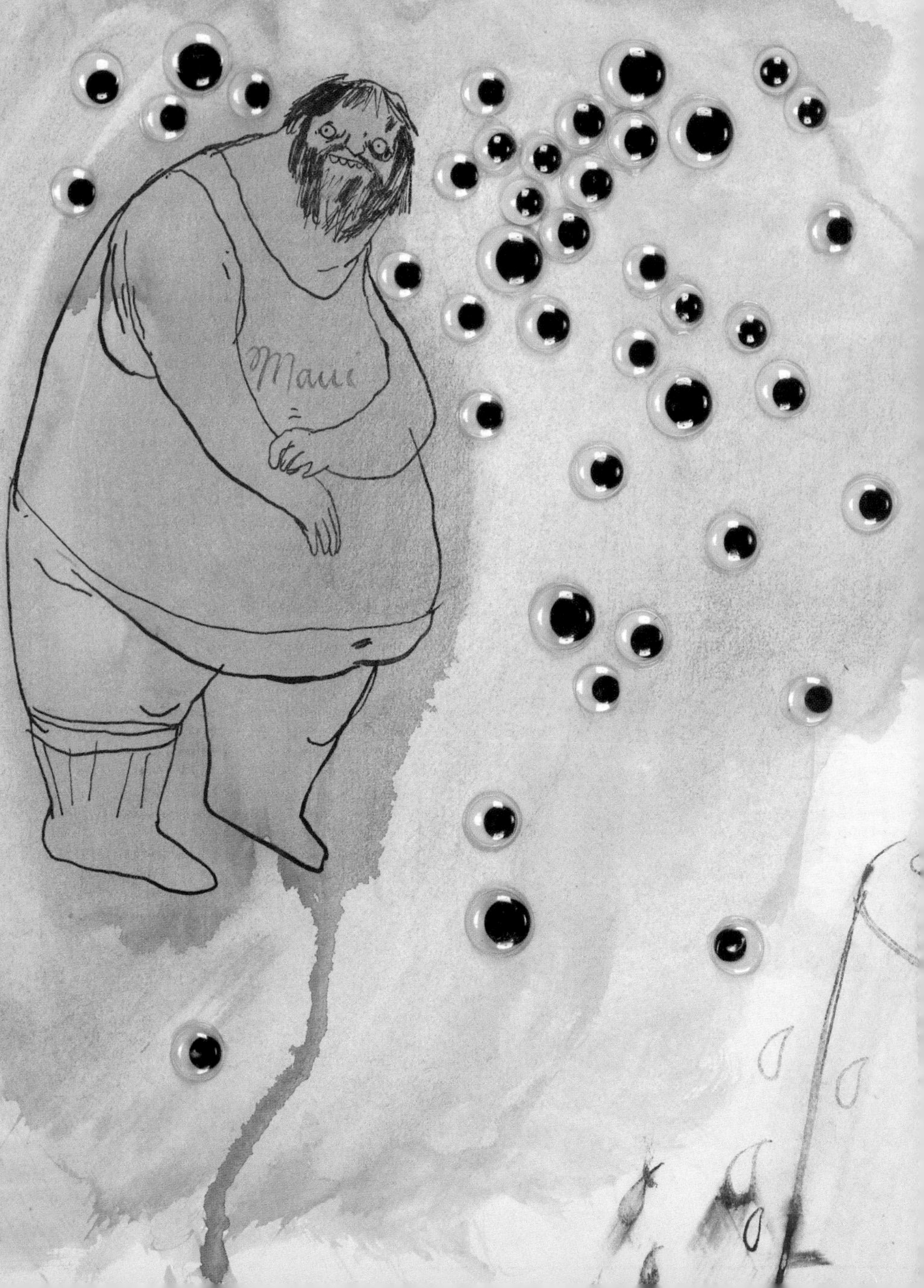
Maui

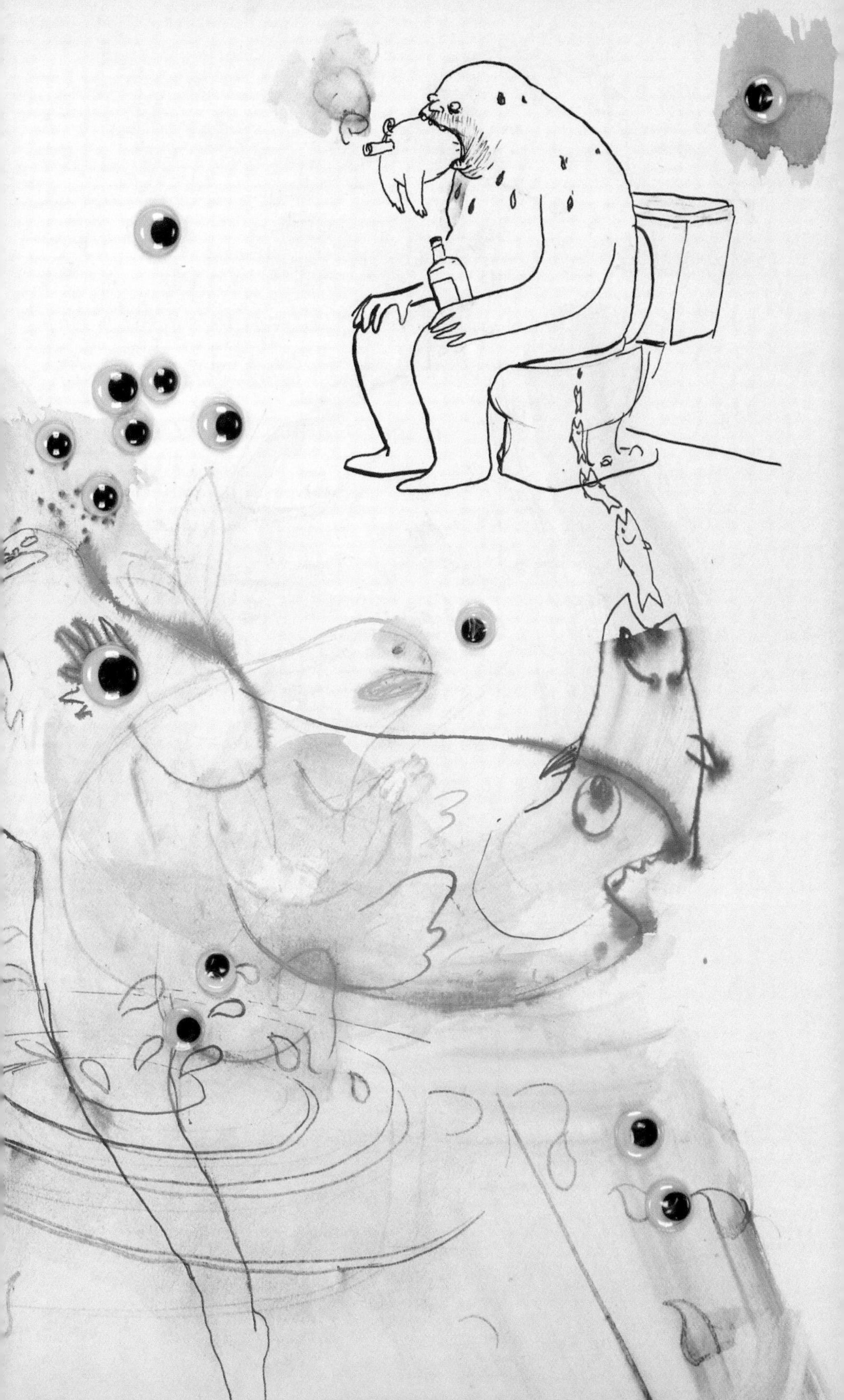

Fast Eddy an' Jimbo the Mook

These guys the best, next time you go by train yard you see if there. You bring six pack and they probably tell you hobo story or two that knock you sock off. I meet these guy once when. I run away.

Oddly I run away from circus to join home. I not know why people do other way around. At circus man stab me with cattle prod and force Bigfoot make balloon animal. I make all balloon animal with sad screamy face as silent protest. Maybe that story for 'n other page, help fill book.

Eddy + Jimbo take me under wing, show me ride rails, how drink floor cleaner, give me bindle of snacks and shivs and give me name Gorgeous Pete. They always complement Bigfoot saying I have pretty eyes and soft hands. Say I they best girl, which silly cause I no girl but I thought maybe they just not so observant or have trouble with nouns. They always friendly, greet Bigfoot by winking and licking lips, also strange but what Bigfoot know? Me have to leave before 'big initiation' they always talk about, Had catch train to Portland. Miss them guys.

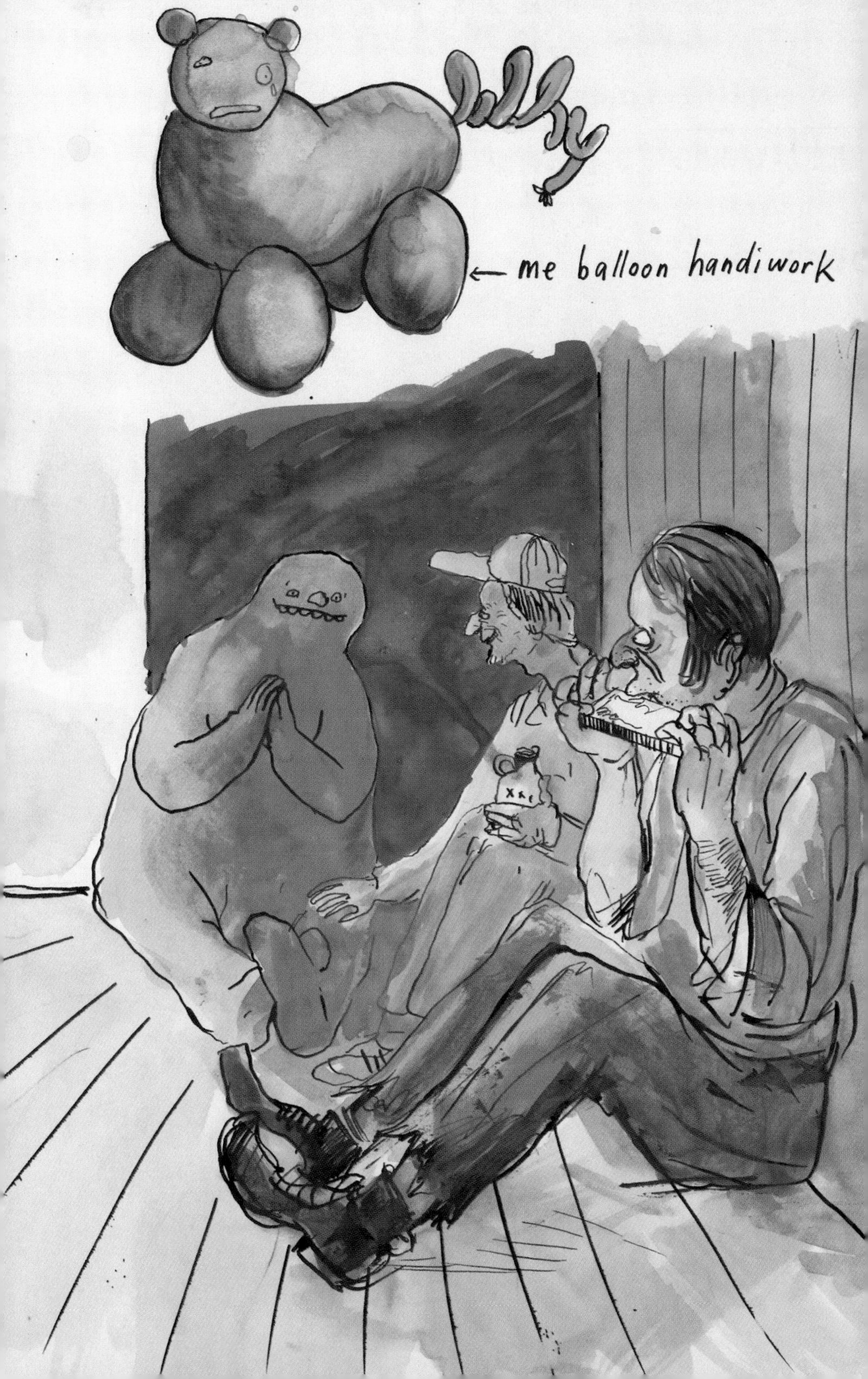
← me balloon handiwork

ROIDS

Because of public profile
Bigfoot under pressure
look good.

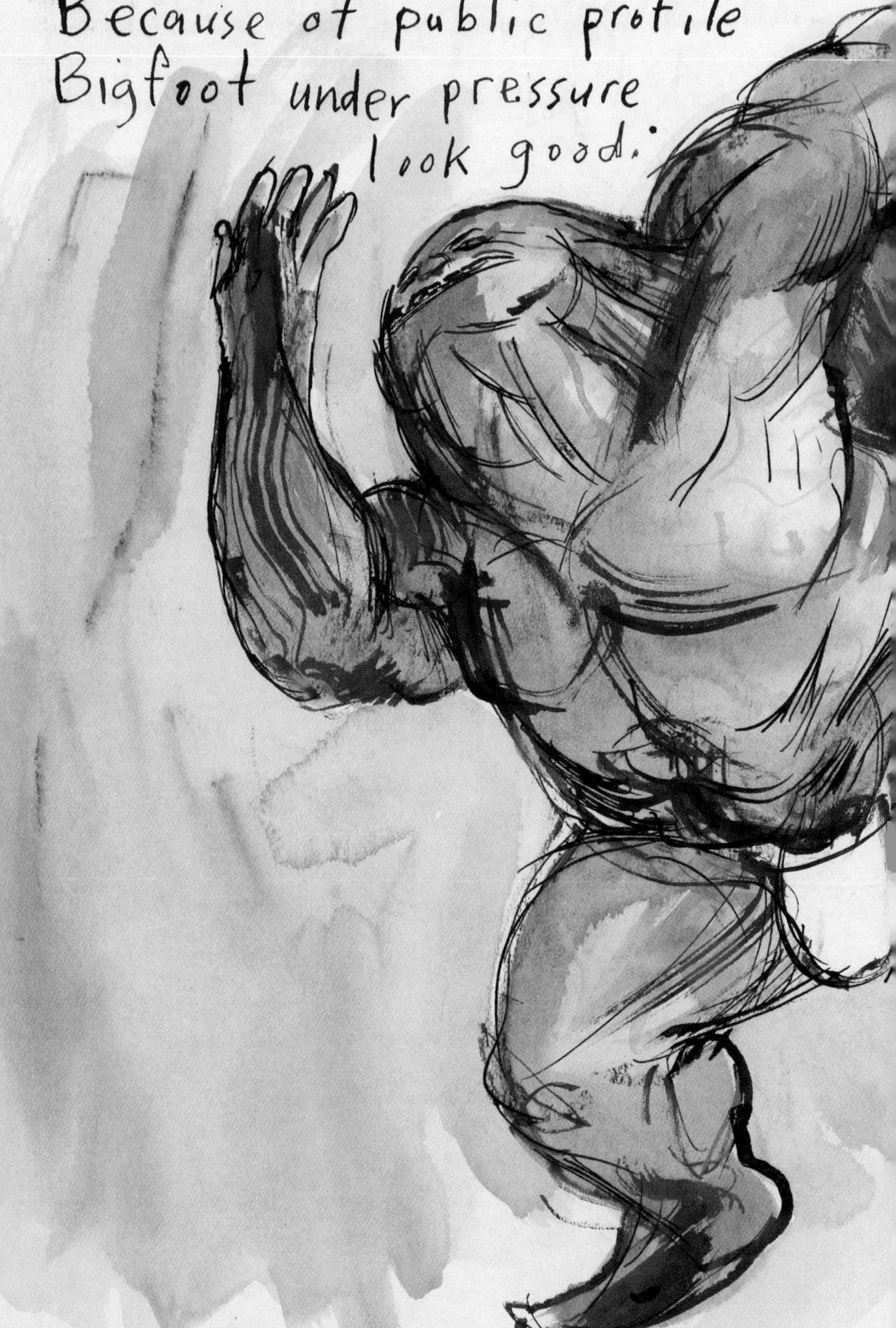

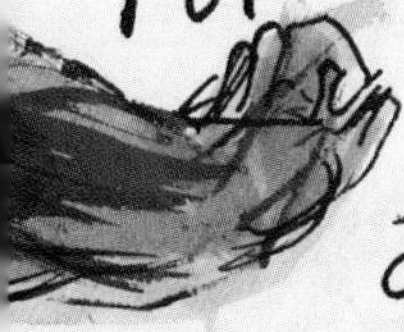

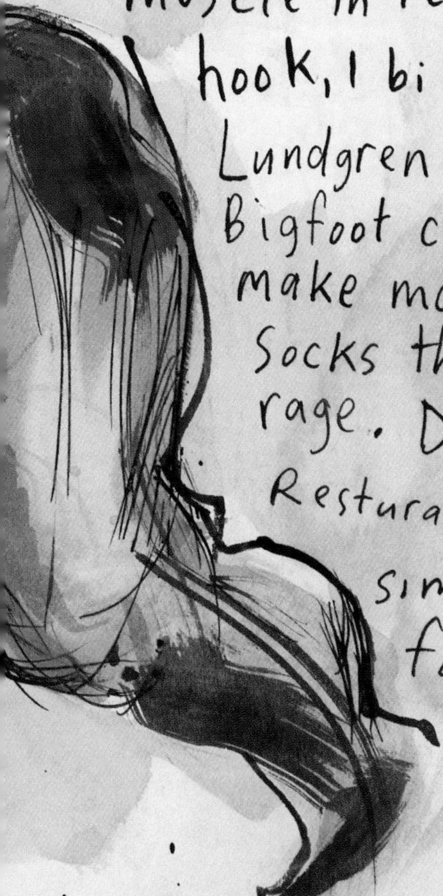

Also have to stay in shape for physical role. At first just want tone up, maybe get six pack. It pain in ass, take too much time, too much work. Start take steroid to speed up process. Soon have muscle in teeth. Phone ring off hook, I billed as next Dolph Lundgren. Drugs make Bigfoot crazy. Everything make mad. One day wear Socks that too itchy. Fly into rage. Destroy Ponderosa Resturant. Only stop when simultaneously liver fail and penis rot off into tub of cruton in salad bar.

Kids, don't use drug.

Whack (Hoot! Hoot!)

Get invitation to high school reunion. No think go. Last one run into Benji. He pick on Bigfoot in school. Make life hell.

Last reunion Benji try pick fight with Bigfoot.

Go outside behind gym. Crowd circle us, say "Fight! Fight!" Bigfoot decide take high road and talk Benji like adult.

Just then owl swoop down from tree and eat Benji.

Everybody think it professional hit.

I niether deny nor confirm.

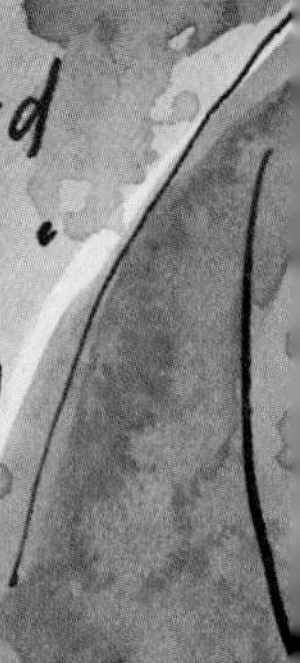

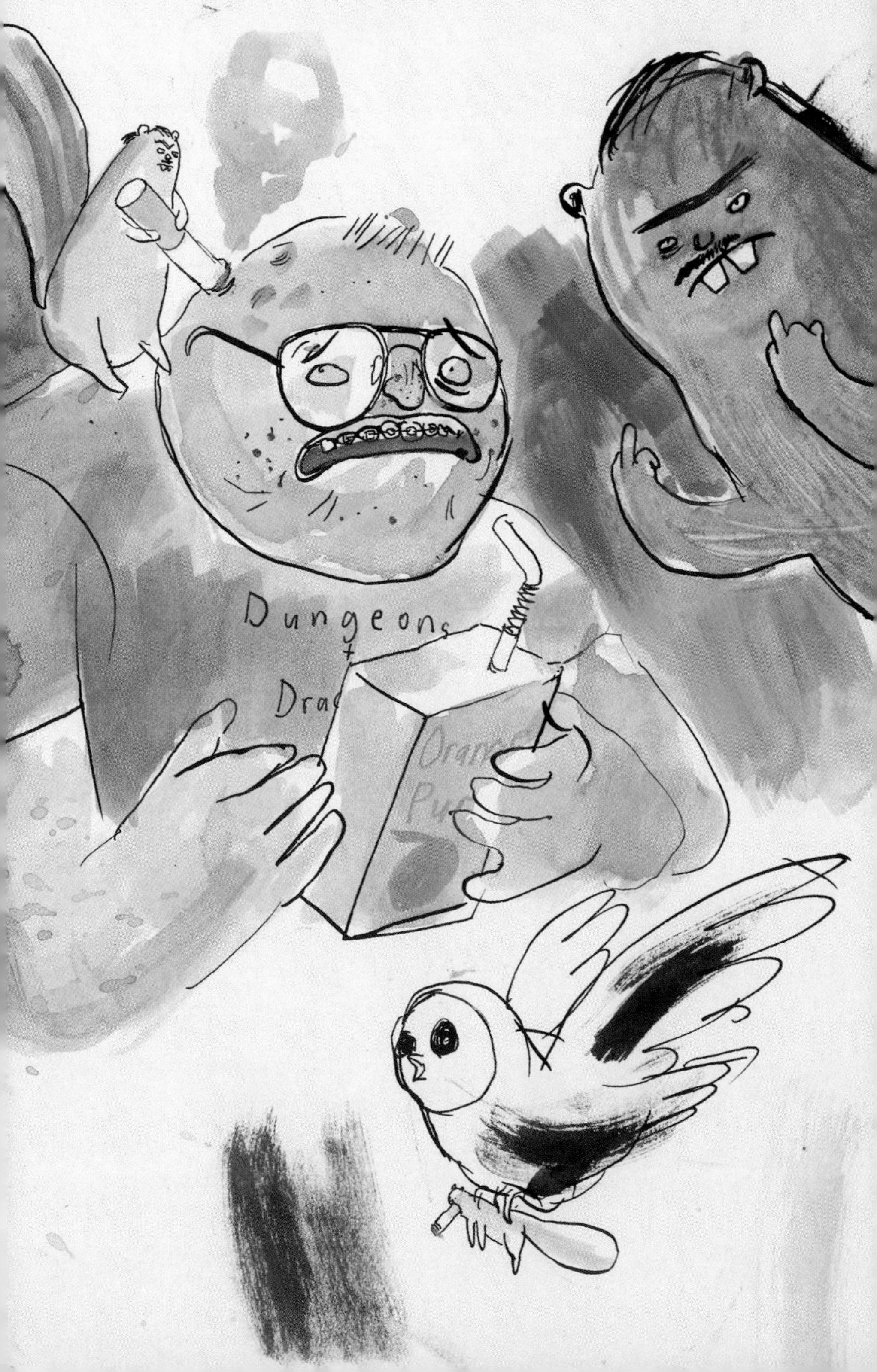
Dungeons
+
Dra
Orang
Pu

Can you Tell Me How to Get?

When first start out audition for a lot of roles, Agent at tim. think I suited for children program becase I furry and talk simple. Go in try out for role on new show for public television but get beat out by giant yellow bird. Also try out for role of him friend but beat out by freaky elephant. Get angry and throw chair across set, hit this talentless green guy who also no get lead role. Turn out I break him back with chair and make paralyze. He try sue network. He get miserable from not walk and start live in garbage can. Network offer him role as Settlement for lawsuit. Try to get role as garbage man who carry him around but he just scream in terror and hide in can when I around.

So unprofessional.

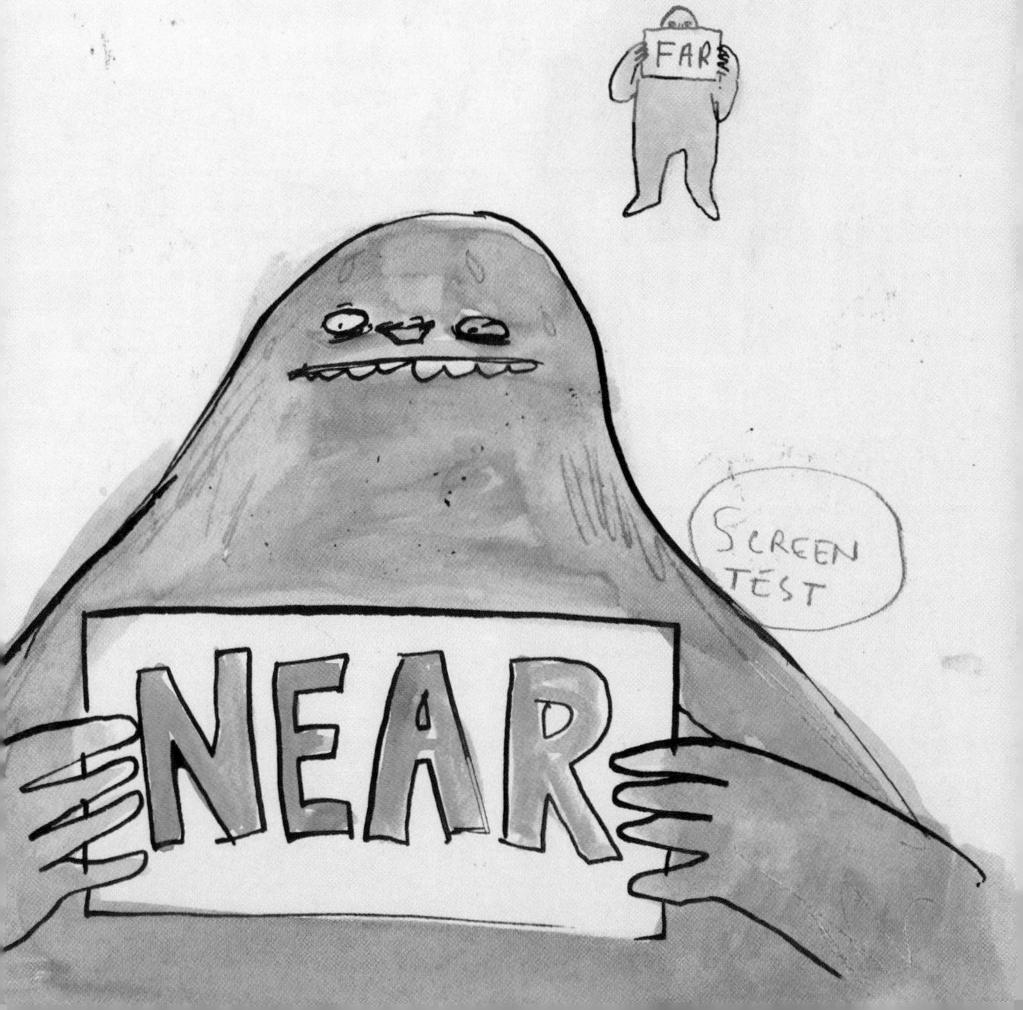
FAR
NEAR
SCREEN TEST

Konichiwa

Like a lot of celebrity I do quick stint in Japan to make some easy cash. Not so voluntary at first. Yakuza kidnap Bigfoot in sleep and make him compete in underground Sumo league where I fight wild animals.

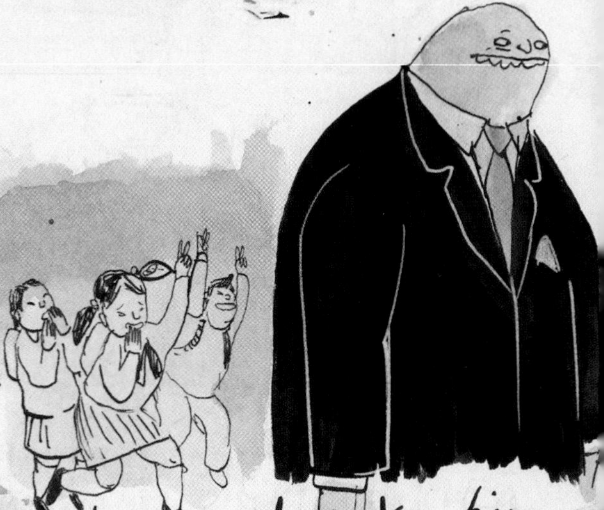

Not want to toot own horn or anything, but I really good. I Harlem Globe Trotter of Sumo. Tear head off puma, throw head in garbage can 50ft. away and pretend play rest of body like guitar.

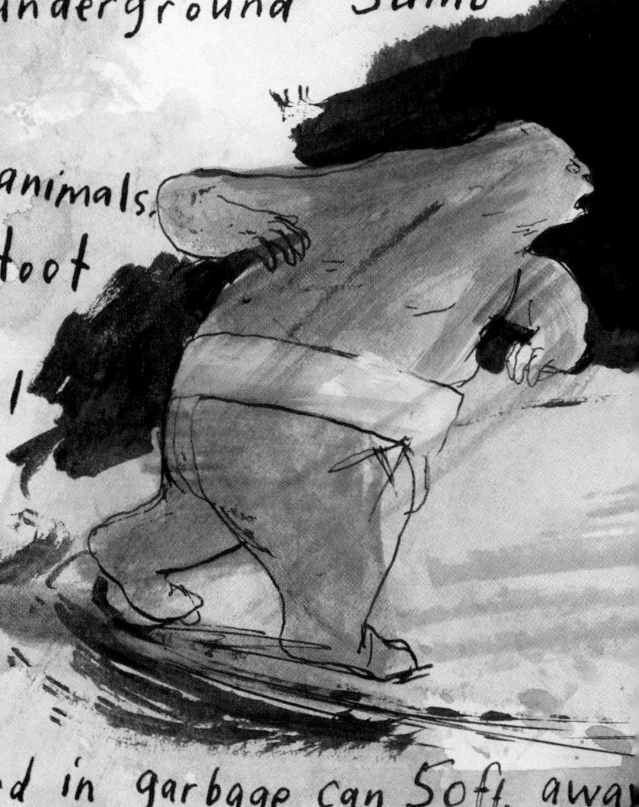

Those stunt make Bigfoot really popular and soon have product sponsor pay lots for Bigfoot endorse stuff.

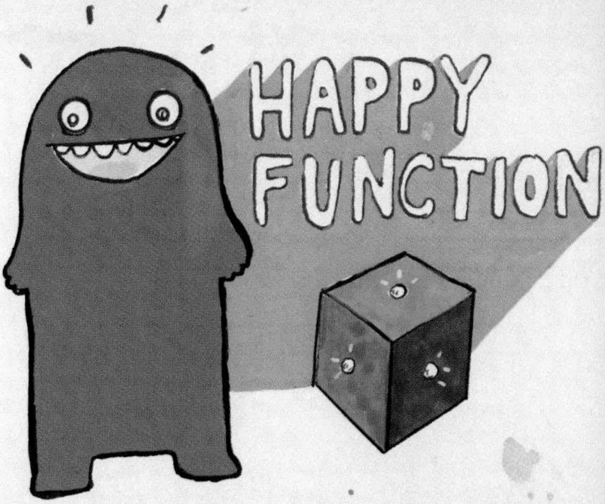
HAPPY FUNCTION

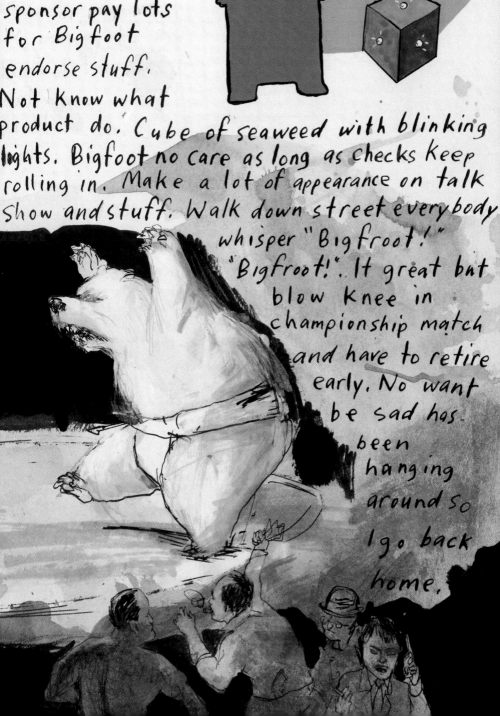

Not know what product do. Cube of seaweed with blinking lights. Bigfoot no care as long as checks keep rolling in. Make a lot of appearance on talk show and stuff. Walk down street everybody whisper "Bigfroot!" "Bigfroot!". It great but blow knee in championship match and have to retire early. No want be sad has been hanging around so I go back home.

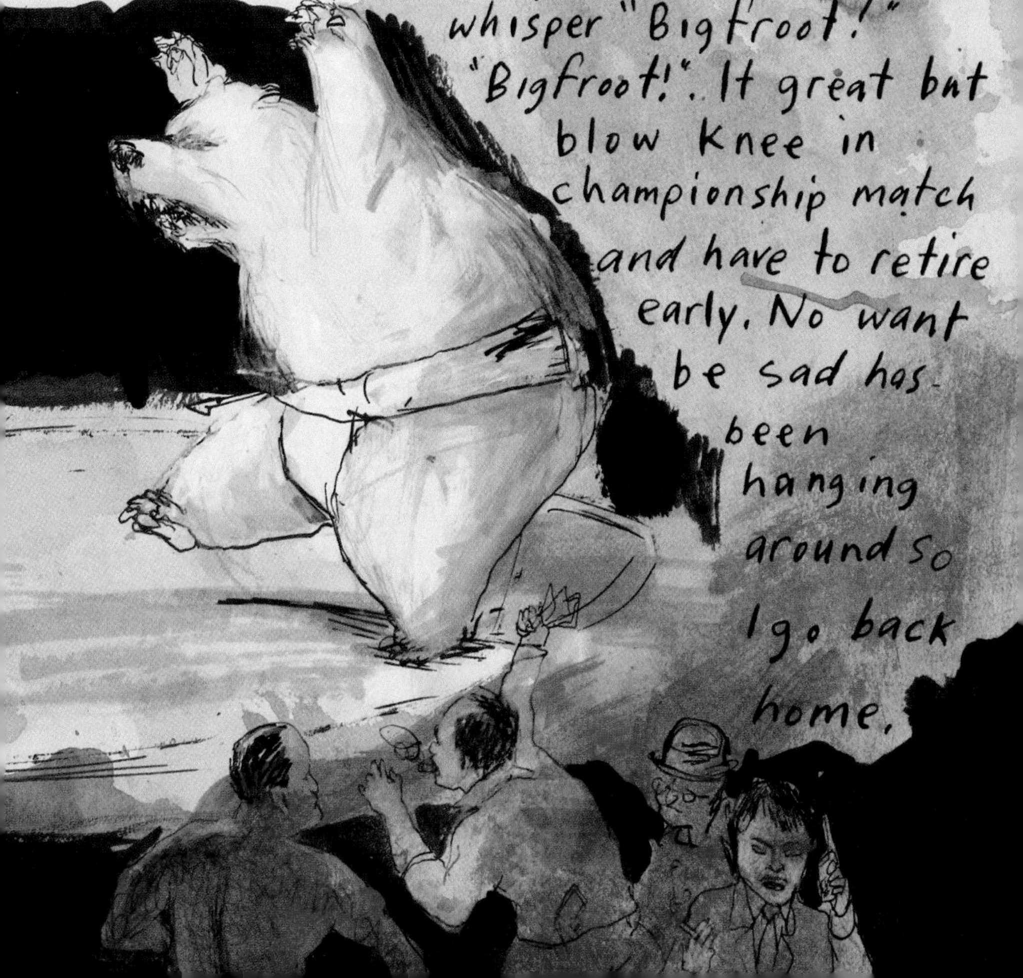

Storytime (Bigfoot aspiring children book maker)

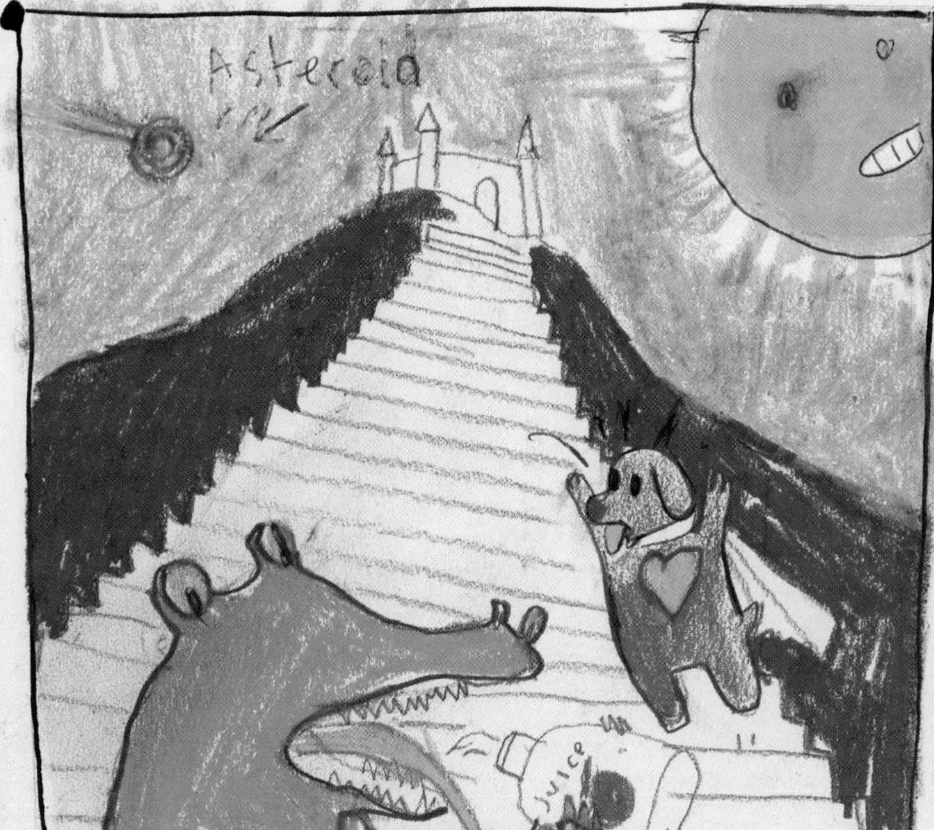
Asteroid
Juice

"It hard climb mountain!" say Sammy Crocodile
"Have keep go or no tomorrow!" cry Mr. Pickles.
"O.k., I love you!" Shout Sammy.

Palsy Pals
And the BIG Discovery.

"So they climb and climb and get to top only to discover it not mountain but computer program to make them think they on mountain. Mr. Pickle turn around say ~~All~~ "When you say you love..." But Sammy not listen because he see ghost that say "All life agony." and then ghost try over and over to suicide but no can because already dead. It then Sammy and Mr. Pickles decide they probably no have should climb mount crazy. So they go home and bake pie and never talk about that day again.

the end.

Skeptic

Why you no belive me?
Why Bigfoot lie about being
abducted by alien?
Even get it on video tape
~~but~~ `expert` say it fake.
Say I stage.
"UFO pie plate" and "Bigfoot
just person in gorilla suit."

Yeah, and this glow
stick in rectum just
get there all on it
own. ████████████

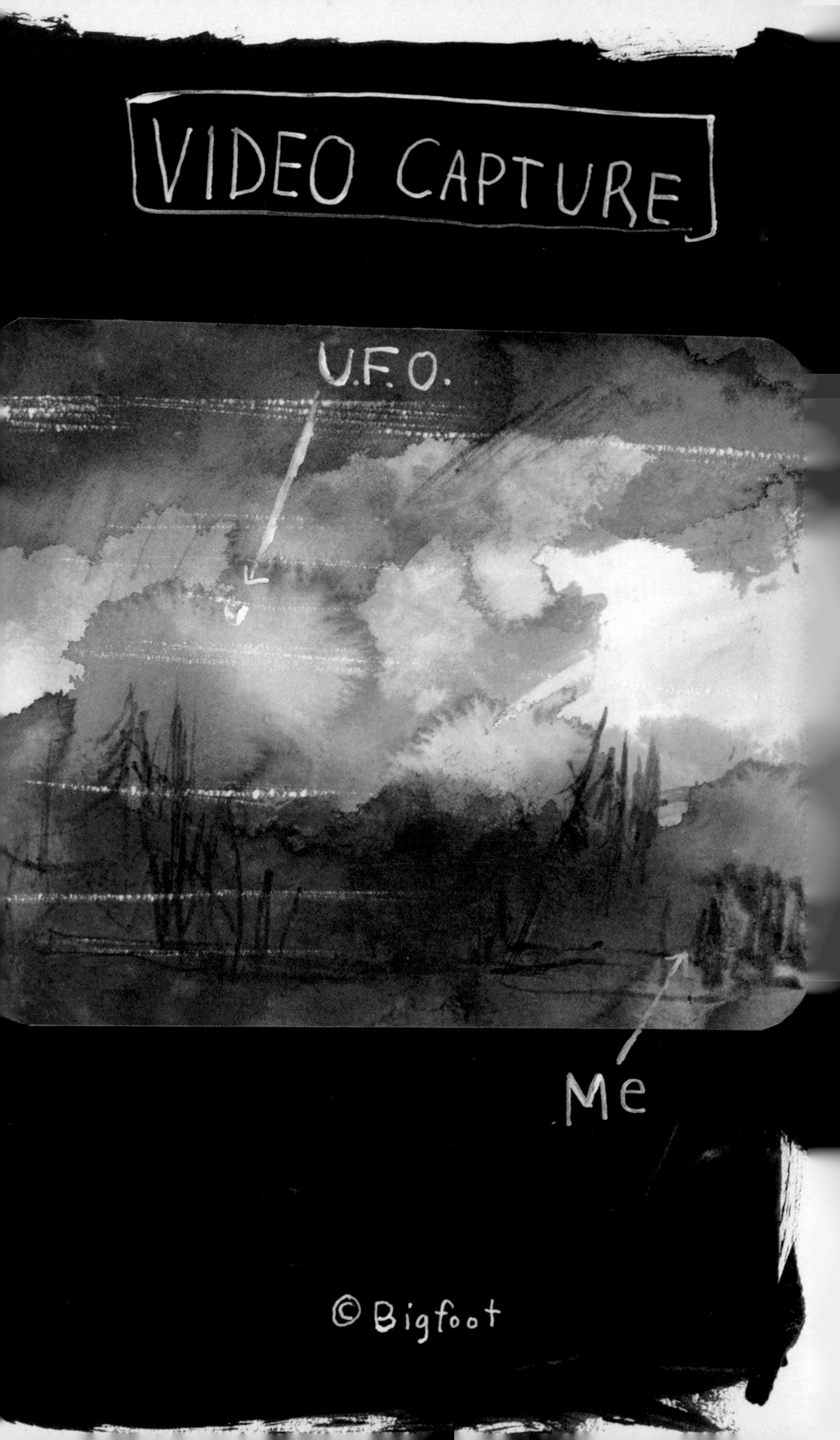
VIDEO CAPTURE
U.F.O.
Me
© Bigfoot

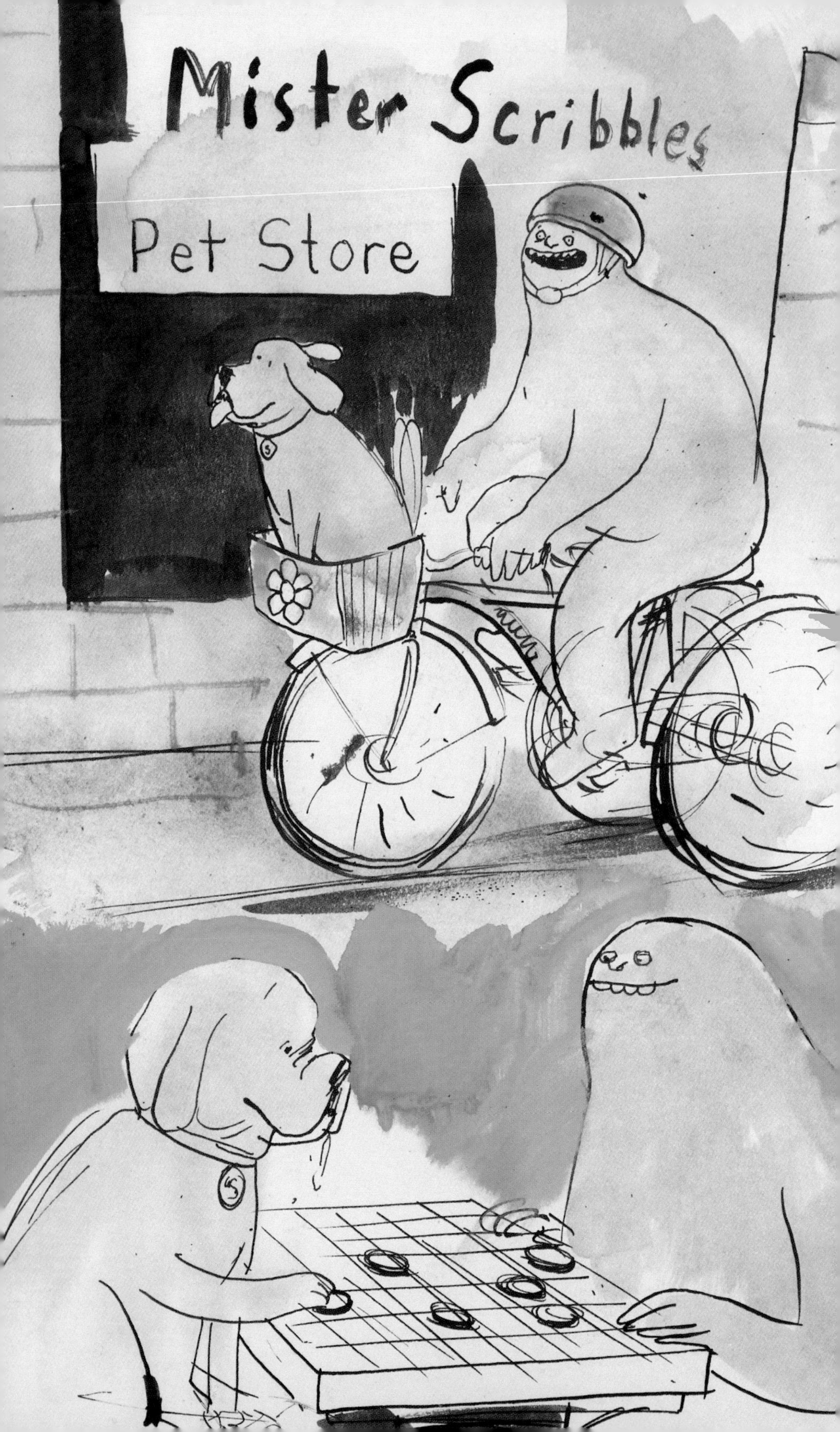
Mister Scribbles
Pet Store

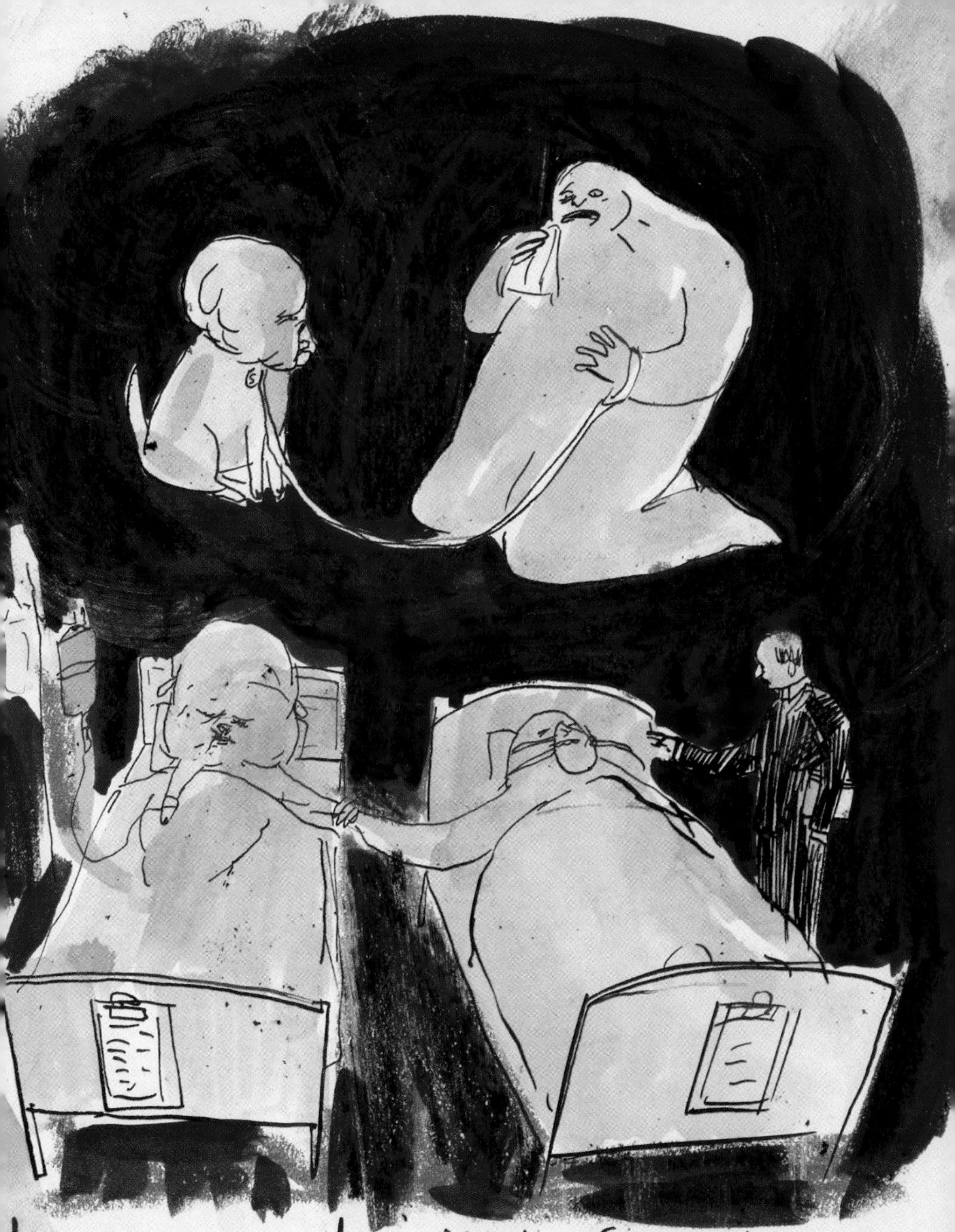

I miss you too Mister Scribbles. Maybe there some devine reason we allergic to each other. Please stop writing letter. Only make miss more. Good-bye Mr. Scribbles.

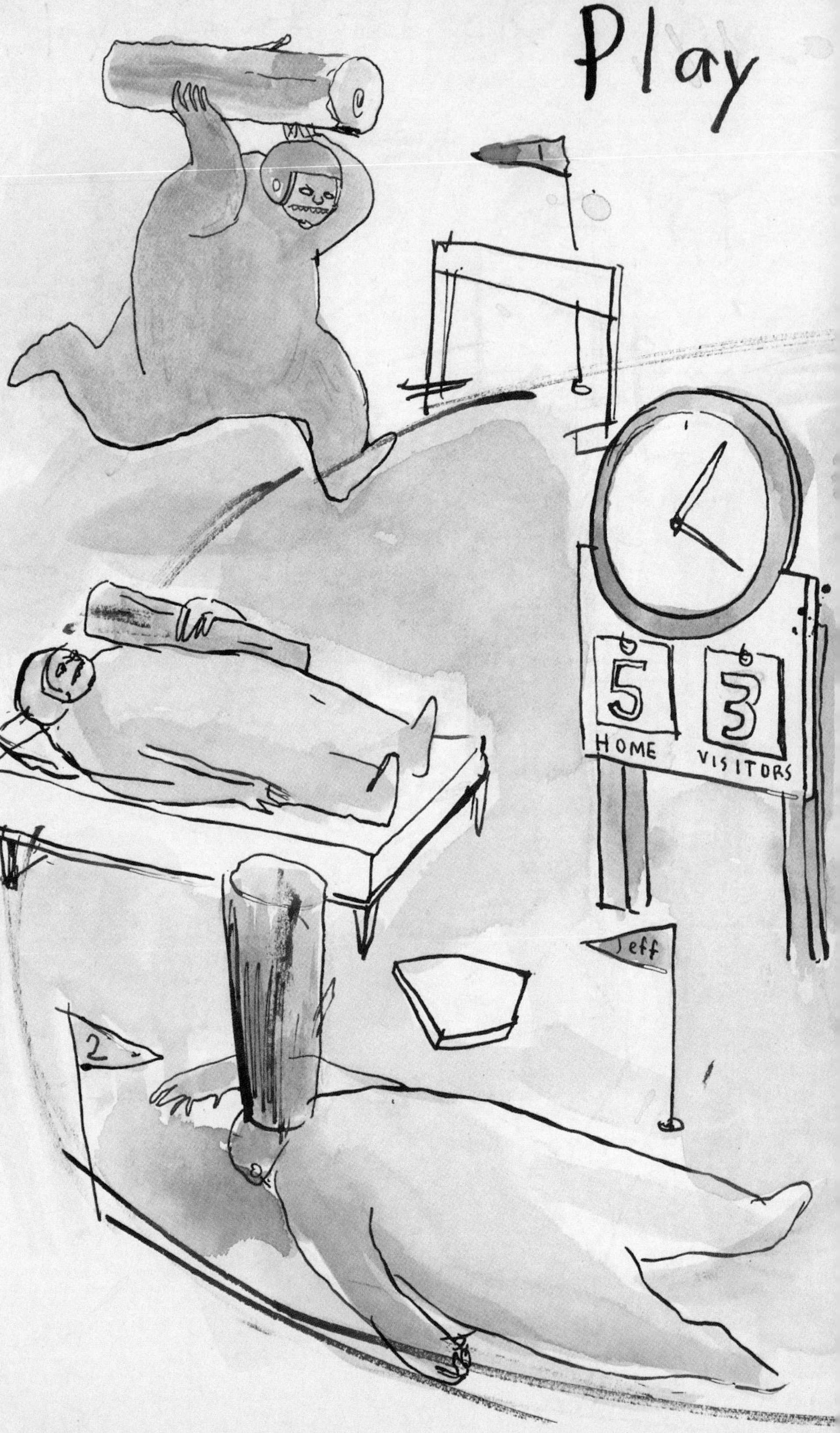
Play
1
5
3
HOME
VISITORS
Jeff
2

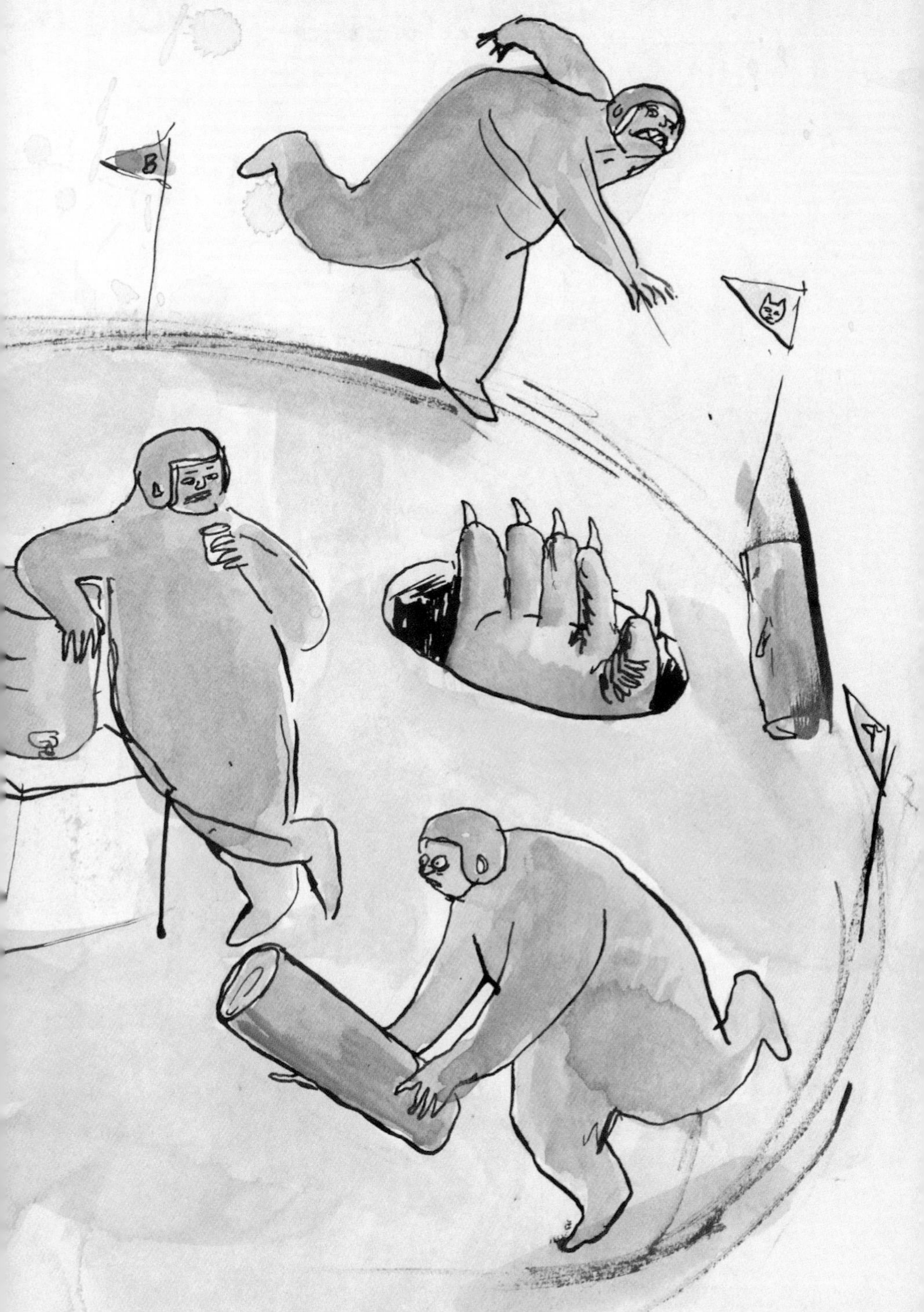

Chuck-Chuck not give character.
It reveal character.

More Than Word

Bigfoot compose rock ballad. Include tablature for clapping. Rock out.

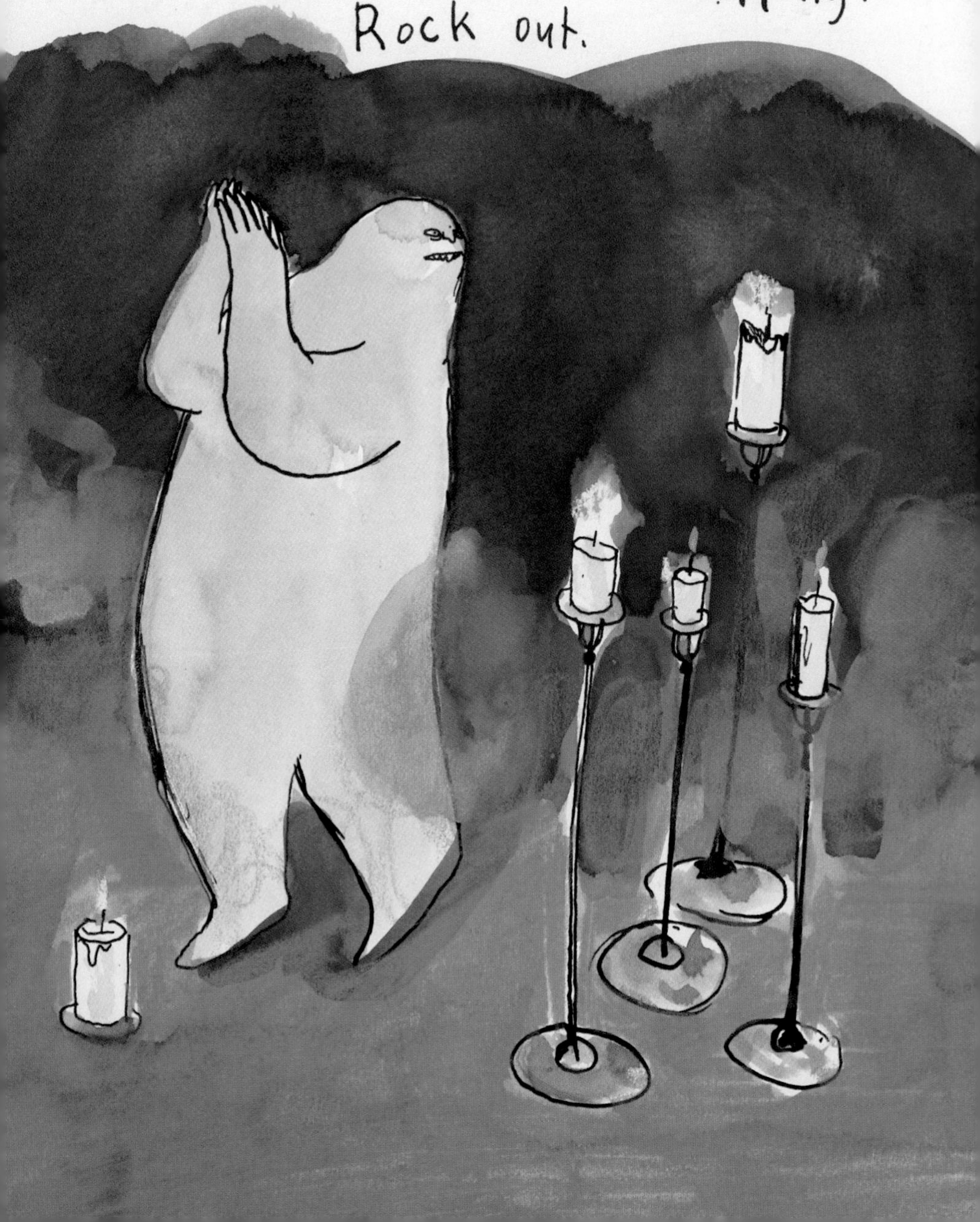

That Would Be Awesome

Music and lyrics by Bigfoot.

Hey baby can you no see there a tear drop in my eye?

Hey baby can you no see you baking sadness pie?

And it hot and it burn when I put it in my mouth

And it burn me insides tooooo

So put pie in window it need to cool for hour or two.

And that would be awesome

Totally awesome,

"Possums are awesome Possums are awesome

But there thunder then there lightening

And wind blow the pie awaaay (repeat)

But if I wish up-on a rainbow

Maybe pie come back some daaay.

✳ 5 second pause ✳
Repeat chorus
7 minute clap solo.

I SANG OUT OF TUNE

You ever see that show Wonder Year? It based on Bigfoot youth, originally called "Grow Up Time Bigfoot." and was make as edutaiment for Romanian orphans. Show concept take off big though right from get go. Fred Savage so cute I could eat head like ripe crab apple. Voice over good too but strange because Bigfoot head voice at time no speak in past tense and not vehicle to carry story with anecdote but severe paranoid schitzophrenia. "Cut out their eyes and hide them in the bread box." was all voice supposed to say but Bigshot writers say it no consistent with show vision. Fuck them. They also constantly Nix Bigfoot idea where Winnie Cooper raging nympho.

Me and the Pheifster

Hell, that only reason any guy ever watch show. When announced show get cancel Bigfoot submit script but get shut down again. Last episode sappy and provide no closure. Bigfoot idea about atomic blast set off by Black Panther much better and lead nicely into Post appocolyptic race war spin off series where Winnie a nympho. Producer Bob Brush probably still kick self. Hindsight 20-20 huh Bob?

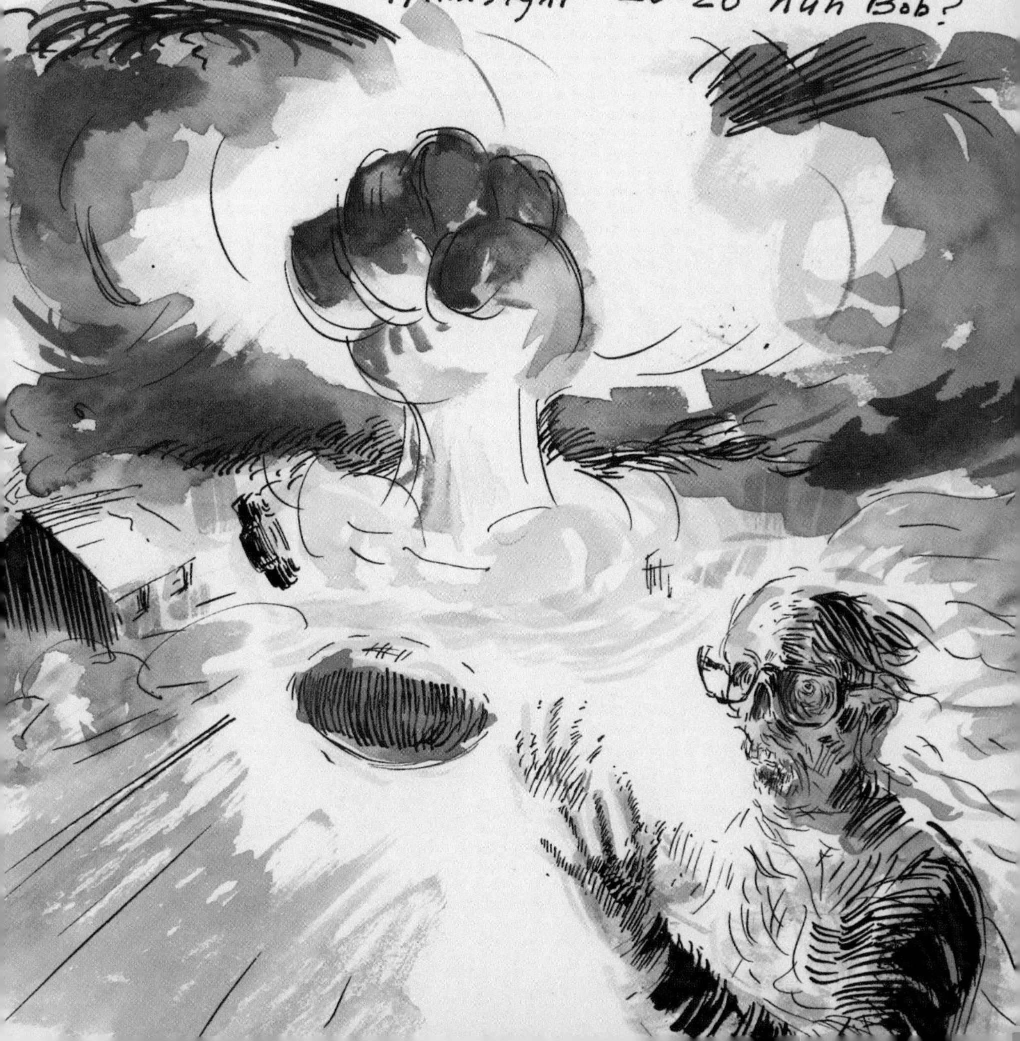

Full of Beans

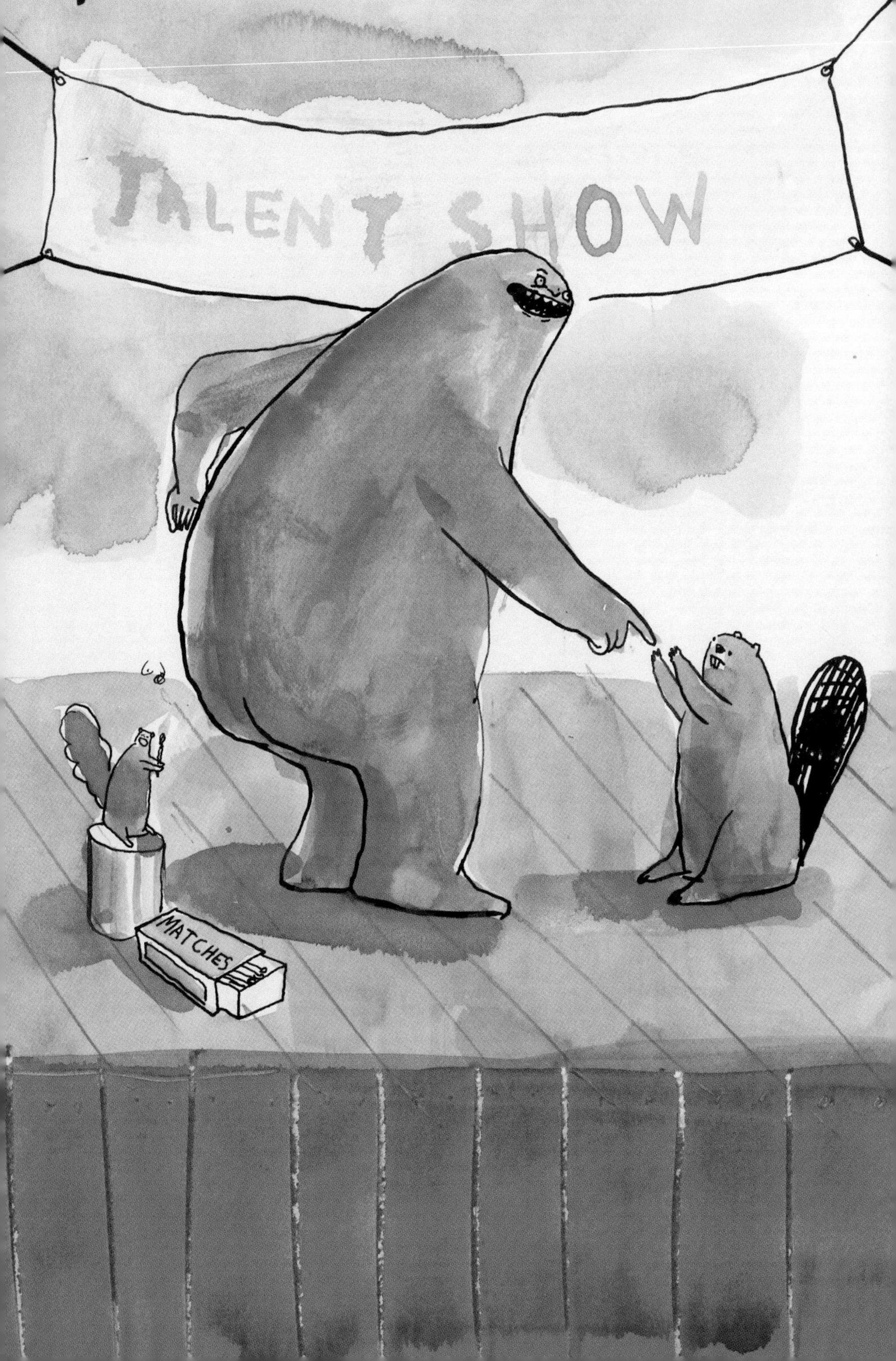

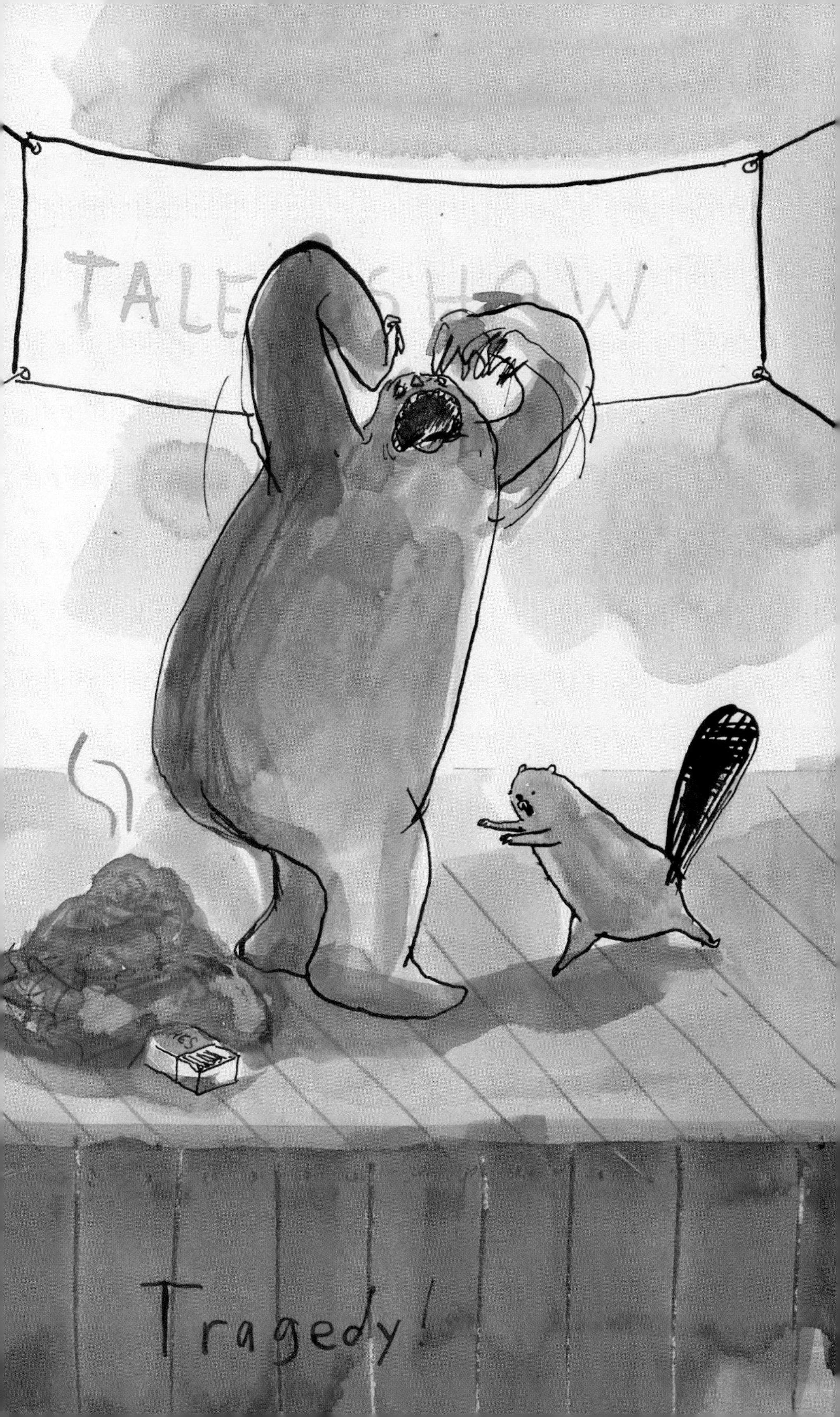
TALE SHOW
Tragedy!

I a Gentle Breeze

Find hard get up in morning?
Maybe say self 'What I doing
with self?': Got no zip?
All morbid obese and cover
in own filth and want die?
What need is copy of Bigfoot
guide 'OUTWARDLY VIOLENT BOOK
OF INNER PEACE."

- Smash away sadness

- Tear low self esteem
  a new A-hole.

- Enjoy simple, delicious
  recipe entire family want eat.

- Smash in happy
  sucess

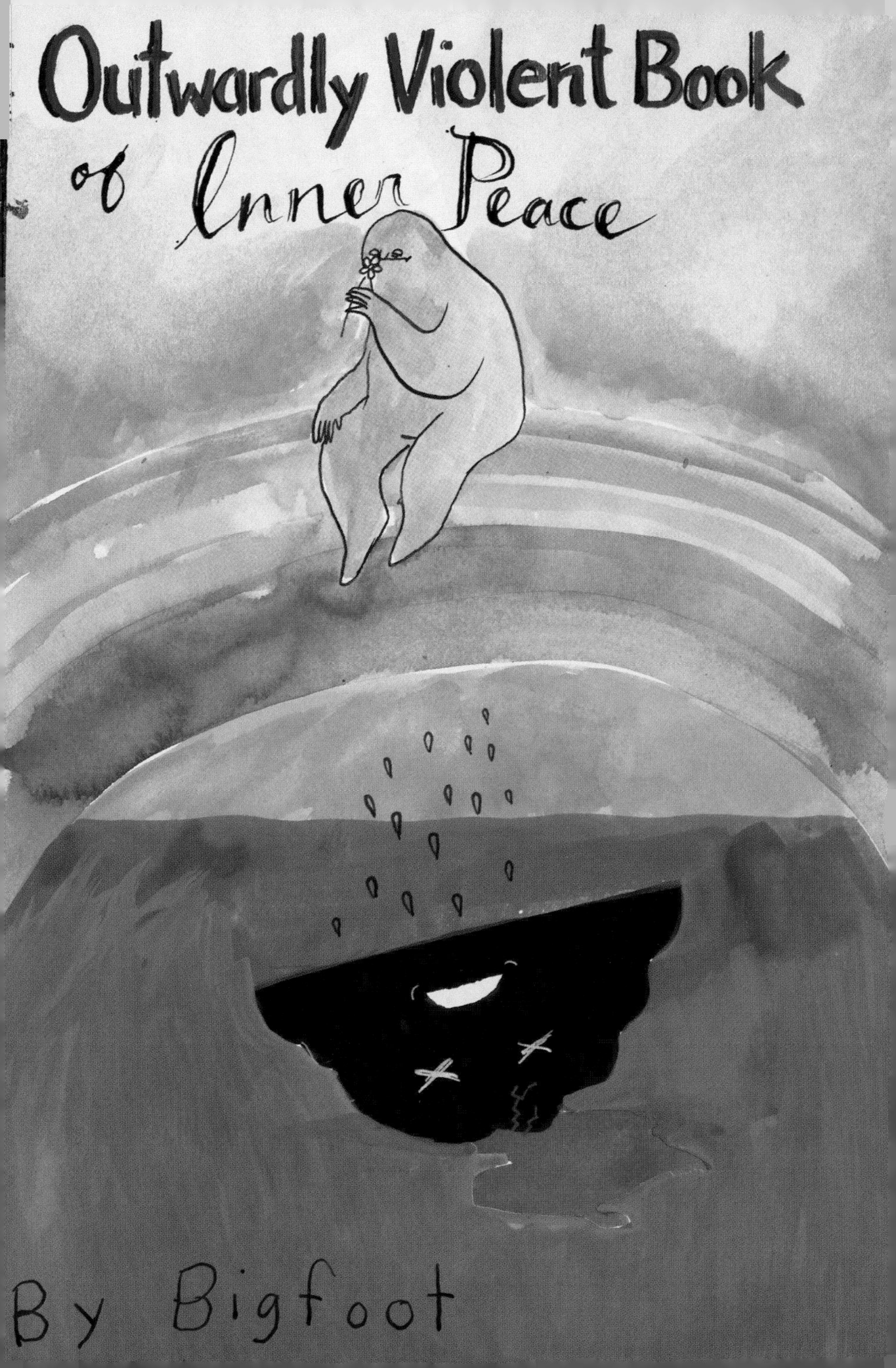
Outwardly Violent Book
of Inner Peace
By Bigfoot

Terrible Dream

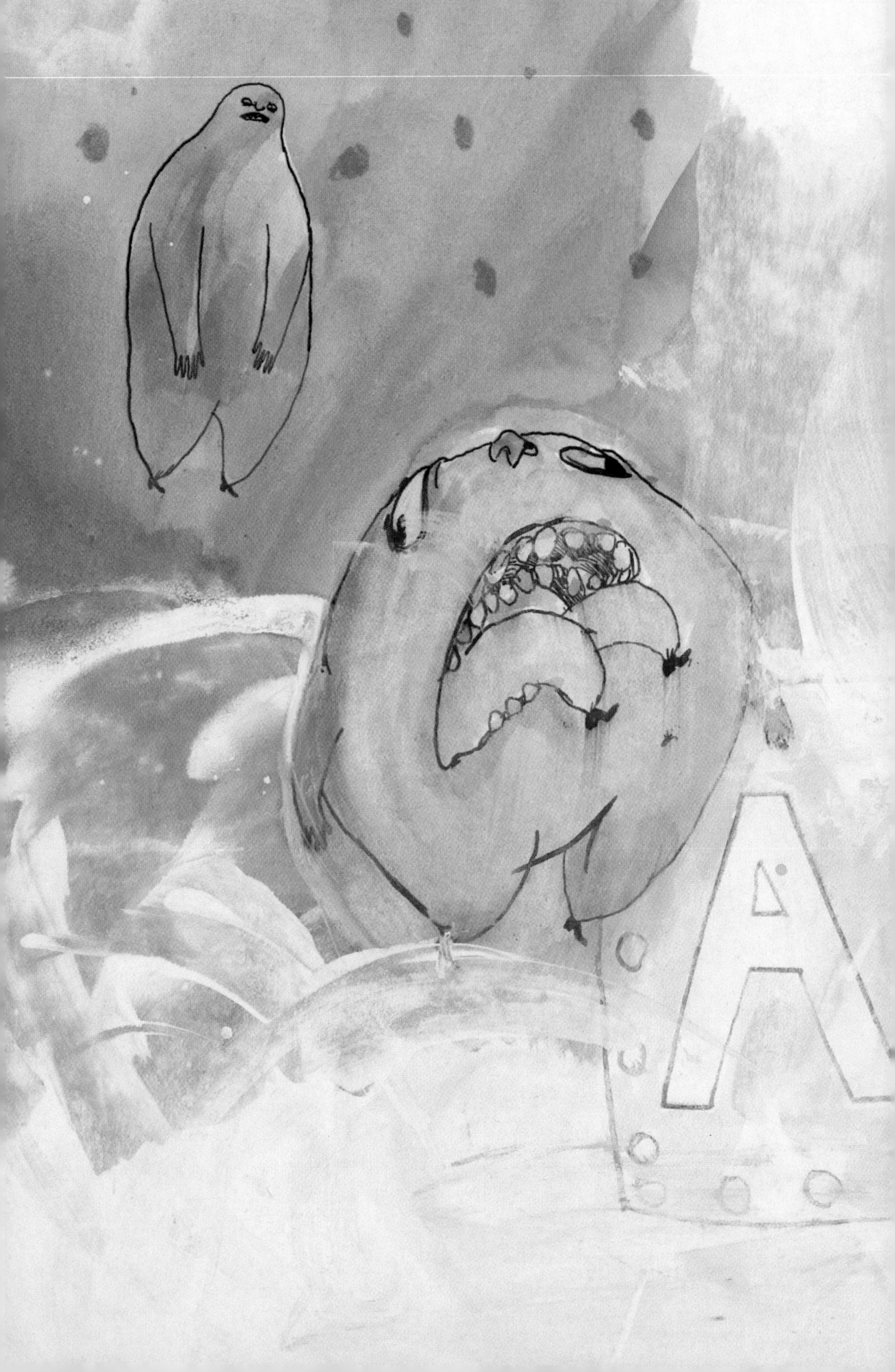
A

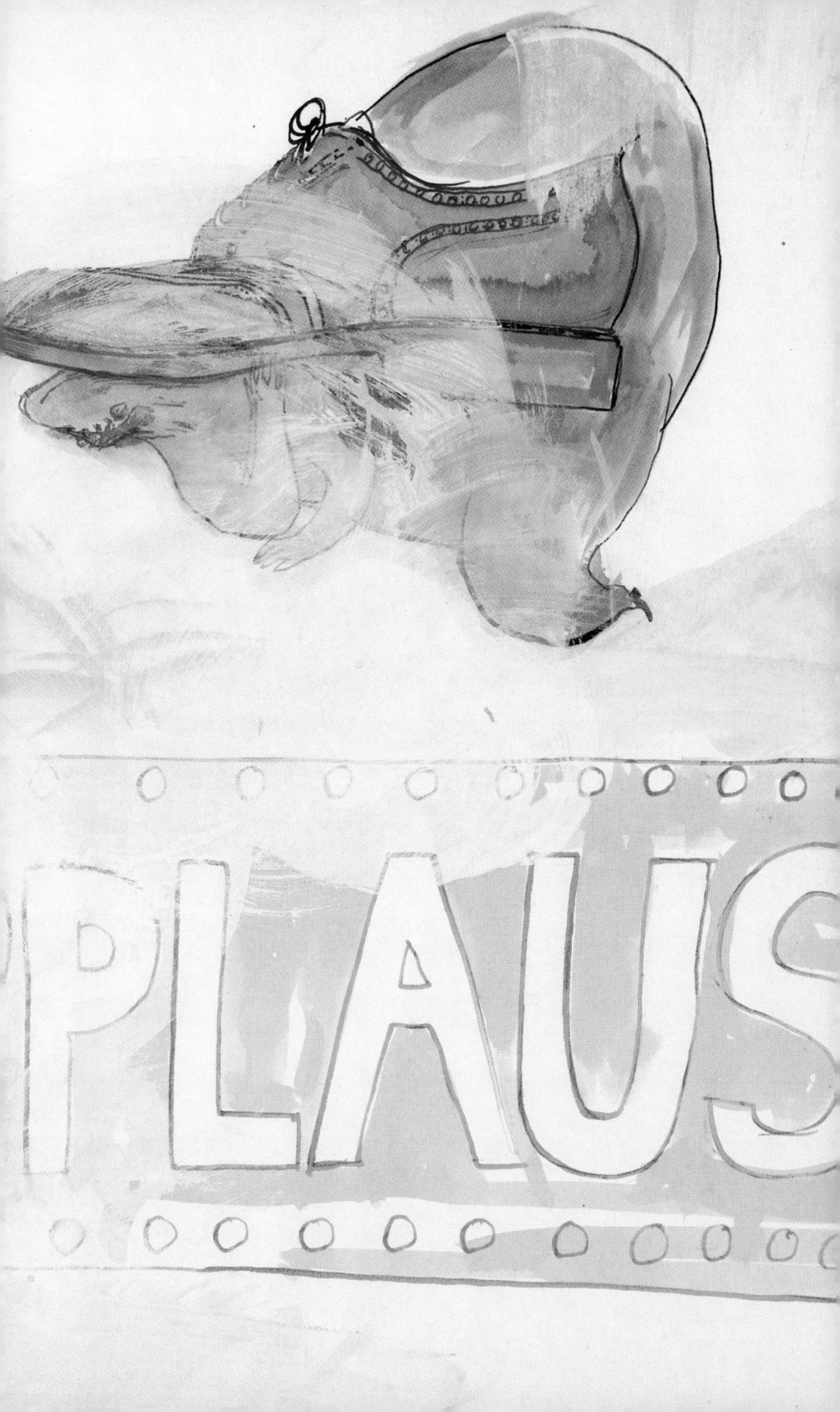
PLAUS

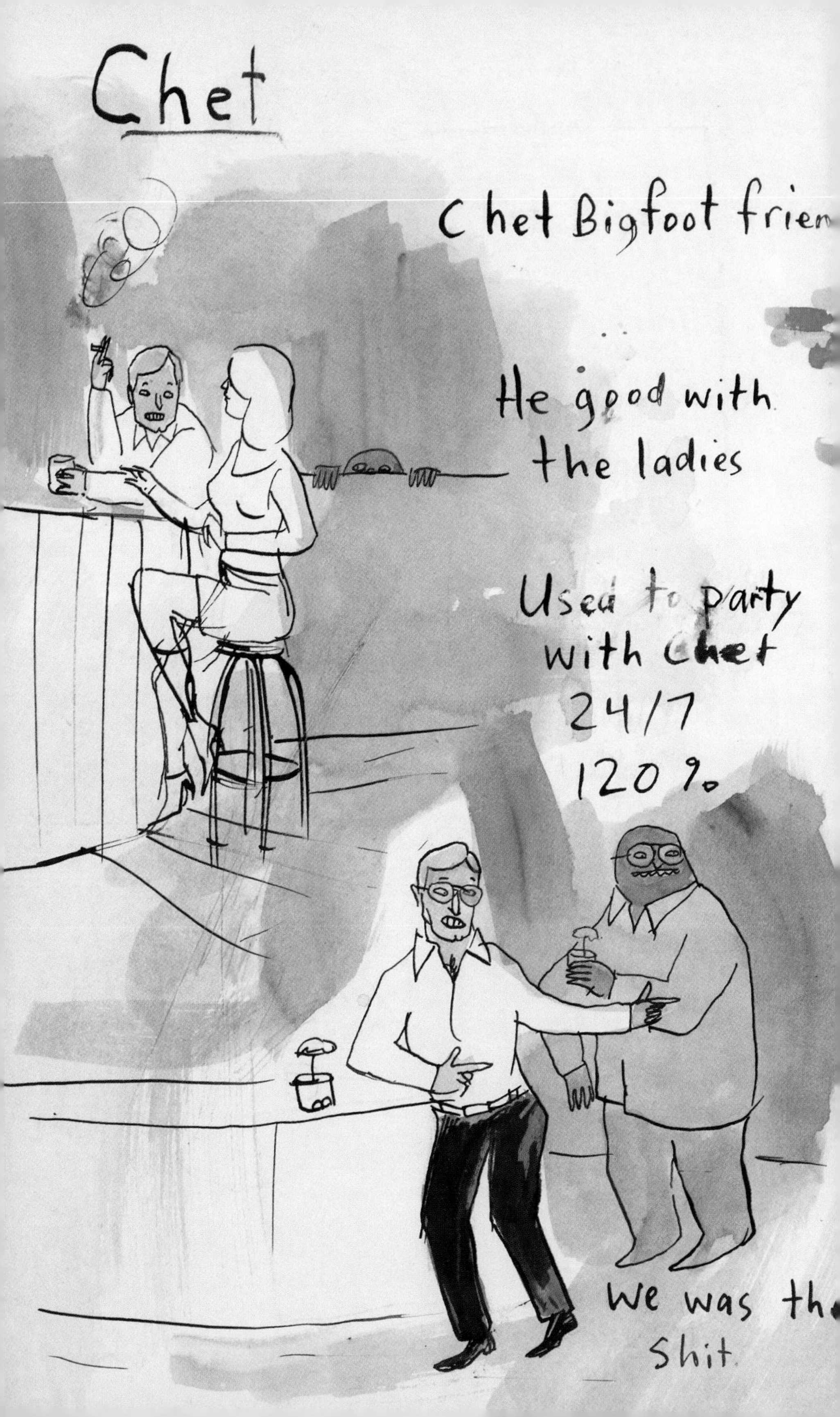
Chet
Chet Bigfoot frien
He good with the ladies
Used to party with Chet 24/7 120%
We was th
Shit.

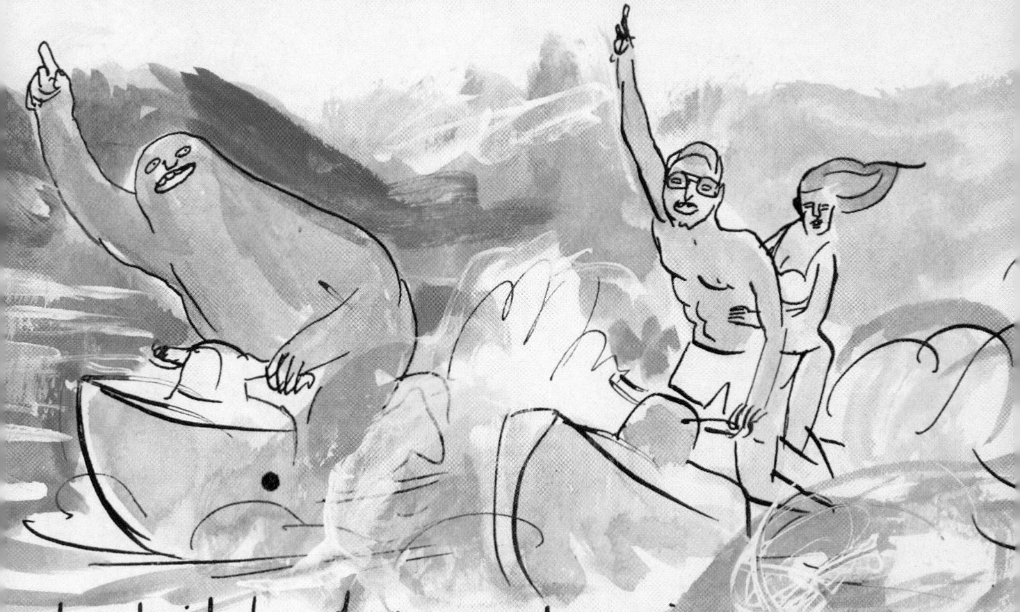

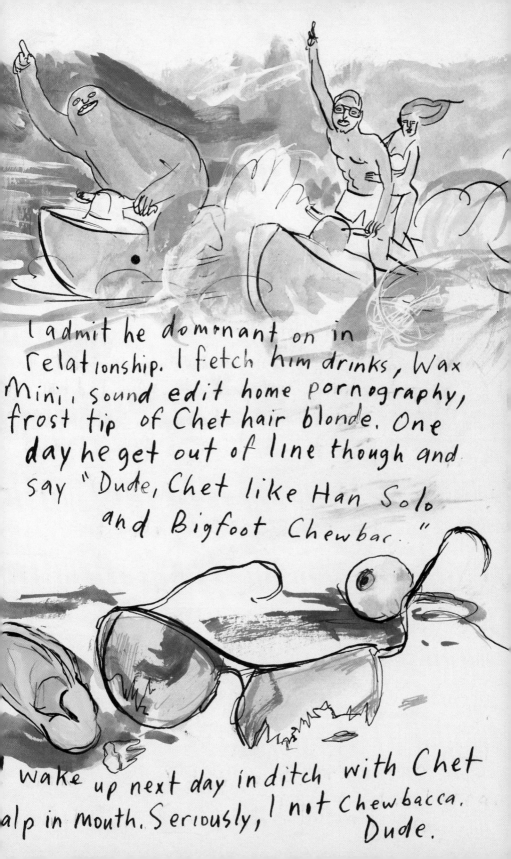

I admit he domonant on in relationship. I fetch him drinks, Wax Mini, sound edit home pornography, frost tip of Chet hair blonde. One day he get out of line though and say "Dude, Chet like Han Solo and Bigfoot Chewbac.."

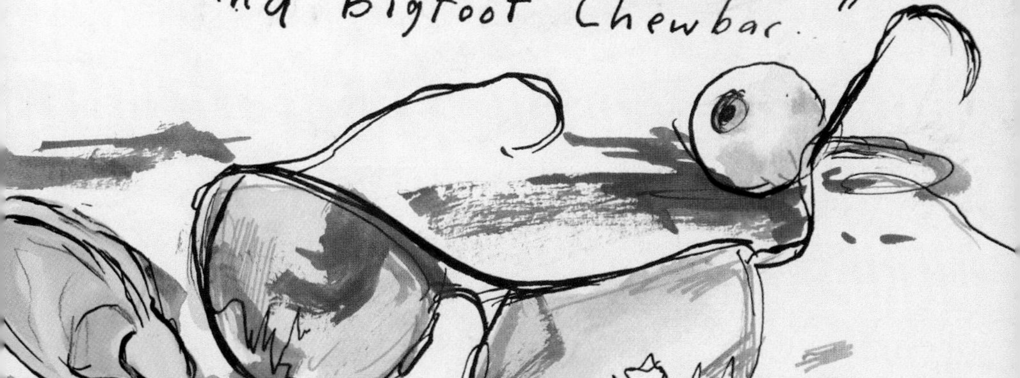

wake up next day in ditch with Chet alp in mouth. Seriously, I not Chewbacca. Dude.

SQUATTERS

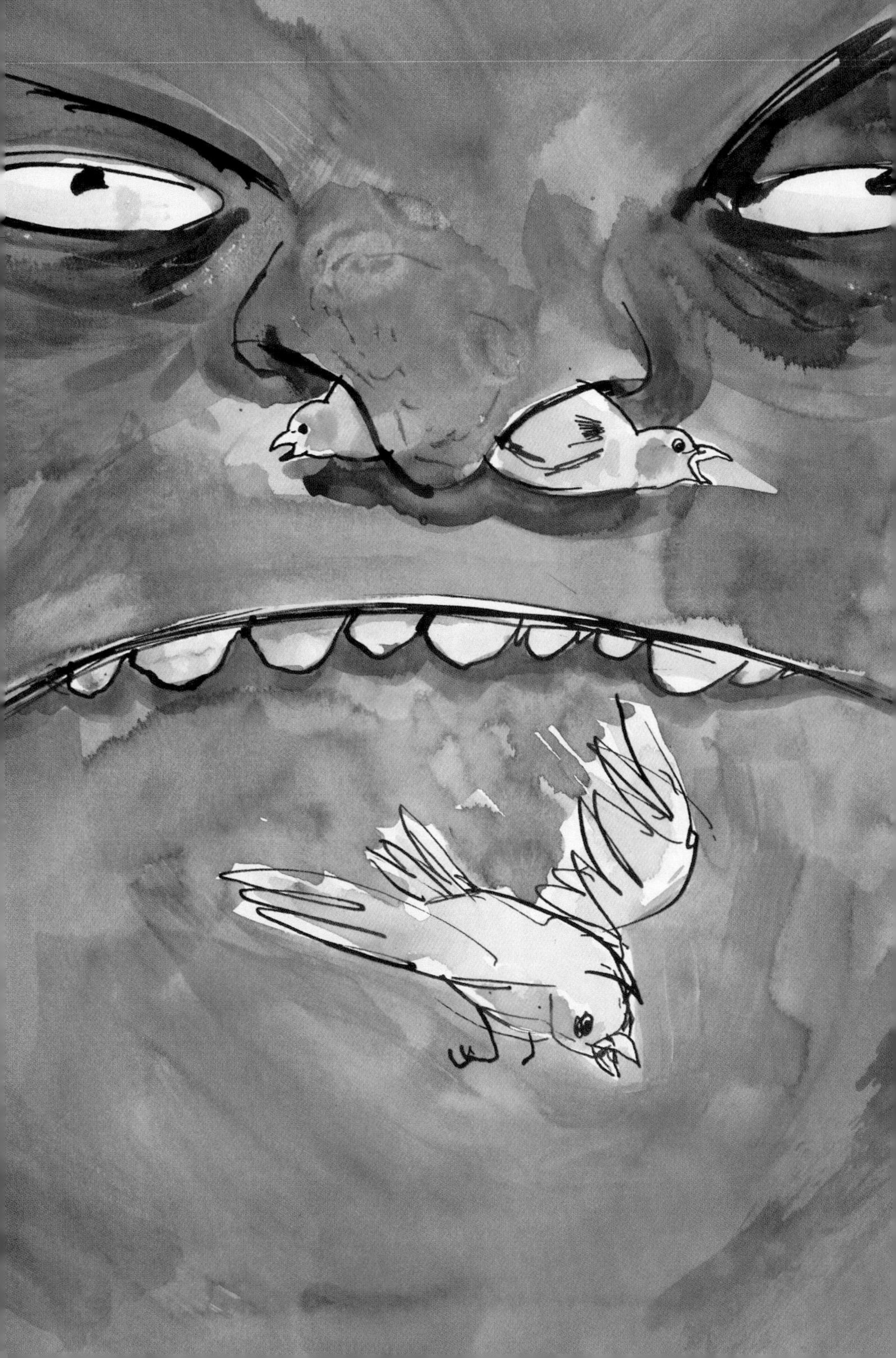

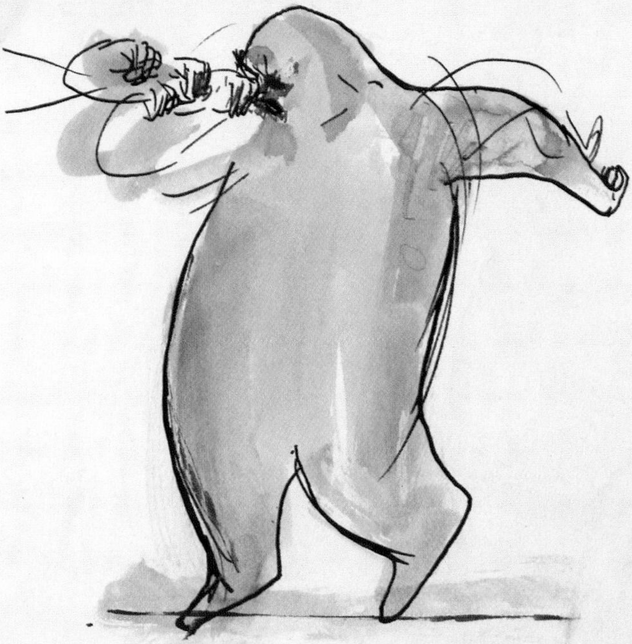

Get out Johansens.

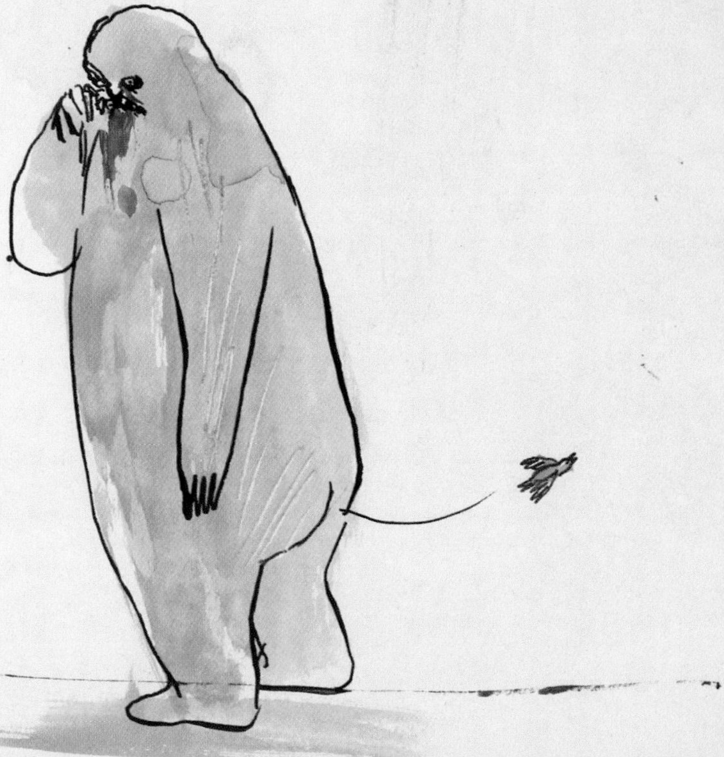

Shush!

Oh, you think I got no skillz? I let you in on little bit of trivia. Bigfoot world only 700 pound ninja.

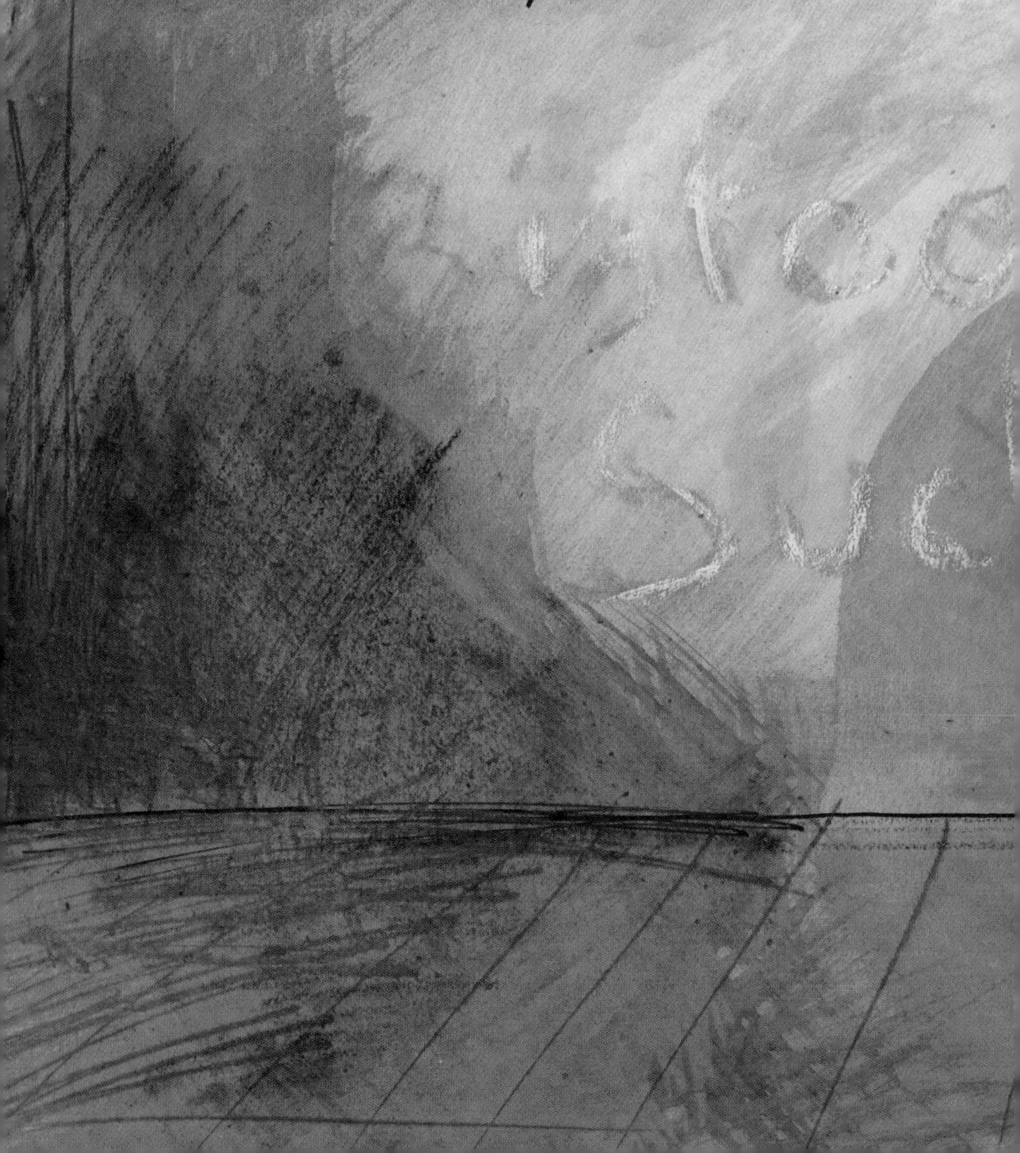

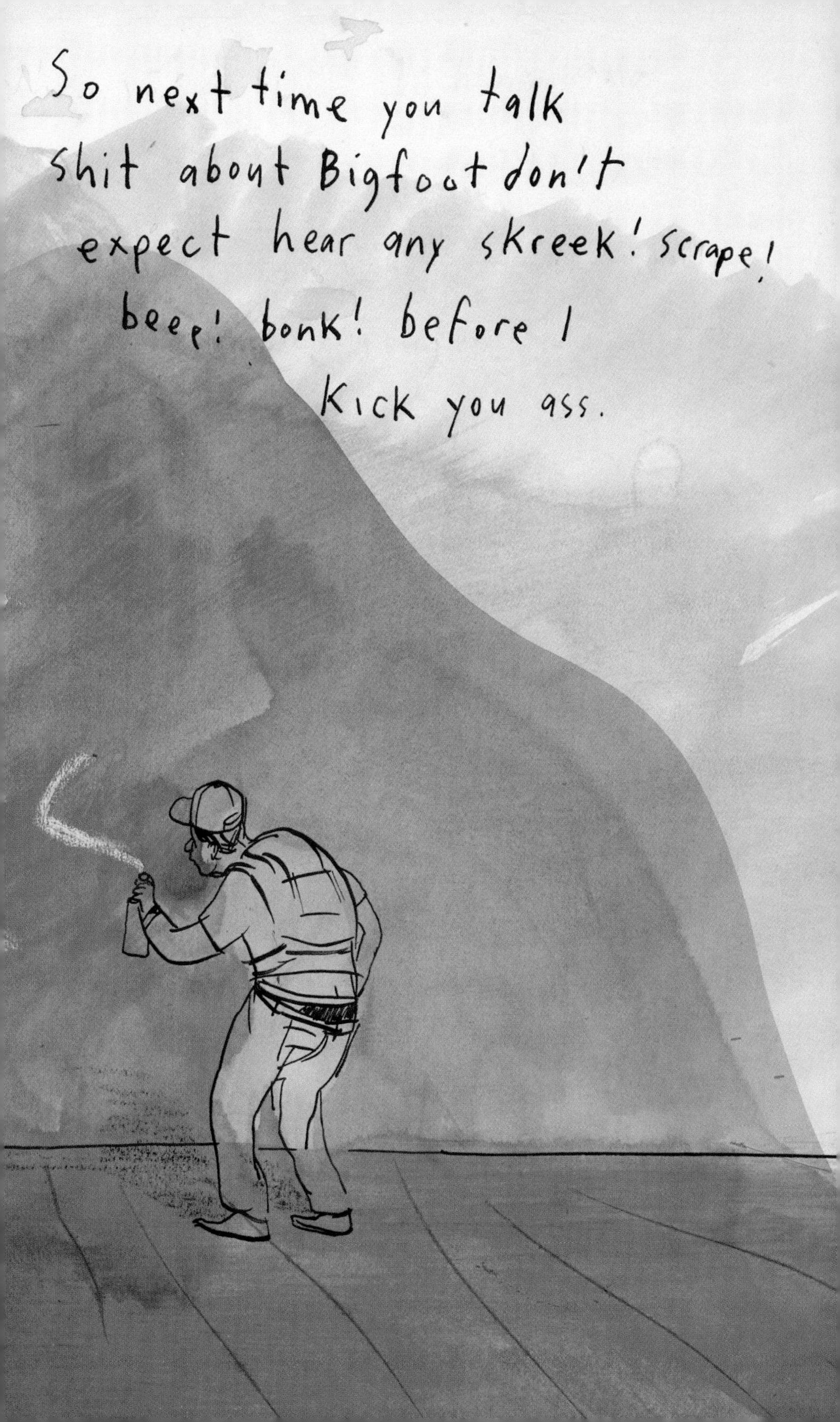
So next time you talk shit about Bigfoot don't expect hear any skreek! scrape! beep! bonk! before I Kick you ass.

Pretty Words

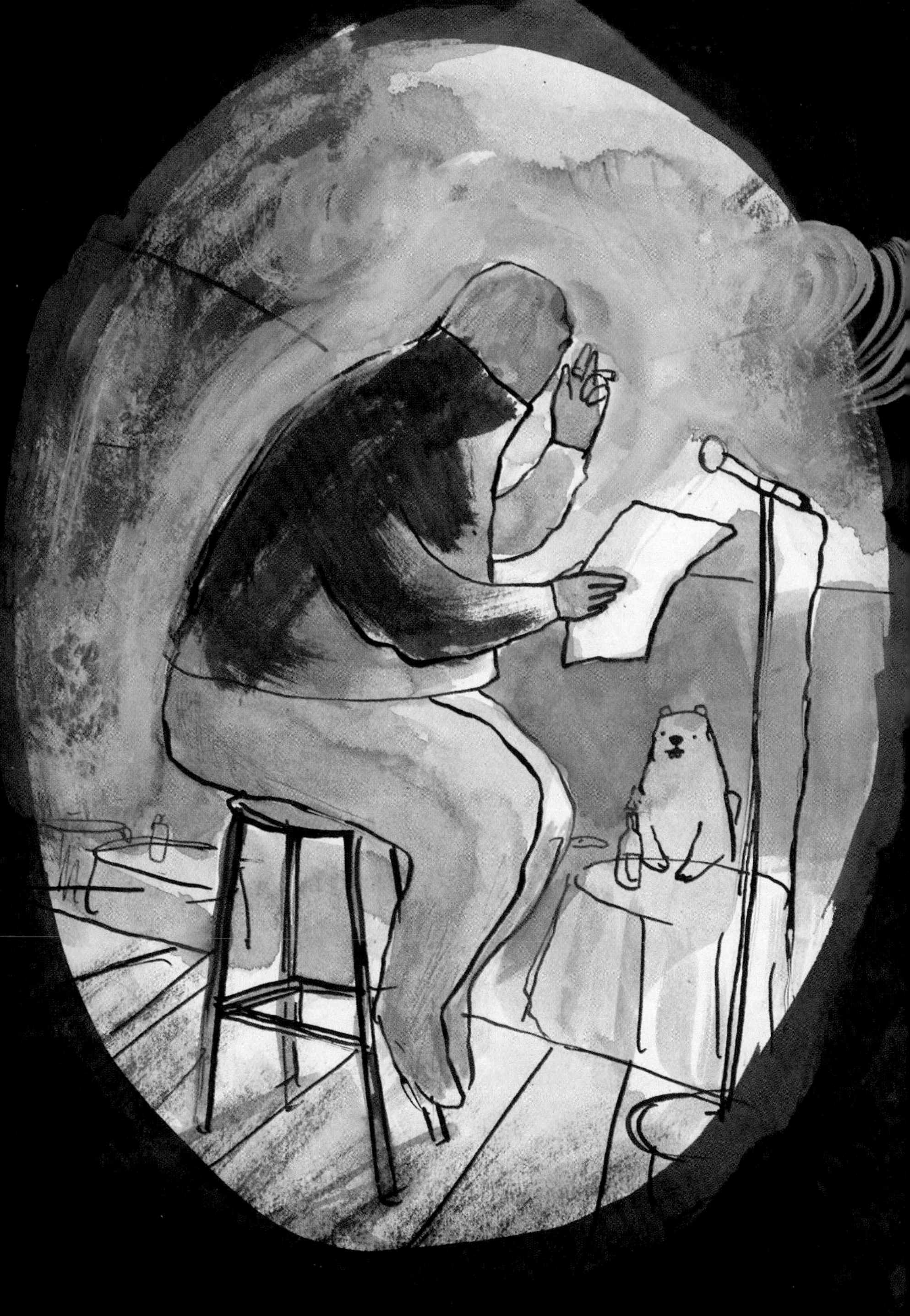

Snooze Button

I pretty sure
That you a robot
Cause when I sneak in you house
And watch you sleep
You sound like broken motor
But when I try fix
You scream like non-robot.

Pardon me.

WORD!

Sunny day,
Sunny day.
I like hot soup.
Warm kitten hug.

So no matter what you do
FIVE-O,
Can't keep a gangsta down.

Once you pop You Can't Stop.

Bigfoot go on big road trip once across America. When hit small towns in mid west food at gas station get worse and worse. Beef jerky with big hunk of corn, hotdog with prizes inside, fudge whistle, drinkable ham etc. Only thing I find maybe worth eat some xtreme-Ranch Jalapeno Pringles. I no never big fan of potato chip but I really hungry so try one and it like taste explosion in mouth. Really, it blow up. All teeth shatter like icecubes. Apparently methylethylbadstuff in chip have violent reaction to Bigfoot saliva, or at least that what doctor tell when Bigfoot wake up two month later. It hard to hear through so many tube + respirator. Want thank public for lovely get well card and such. Very touching. Want say Pringle only have adverse reaction to Bigfoot spit, still fine for human, Please Mr. Pringle, please no sue. You salty treat delicious.

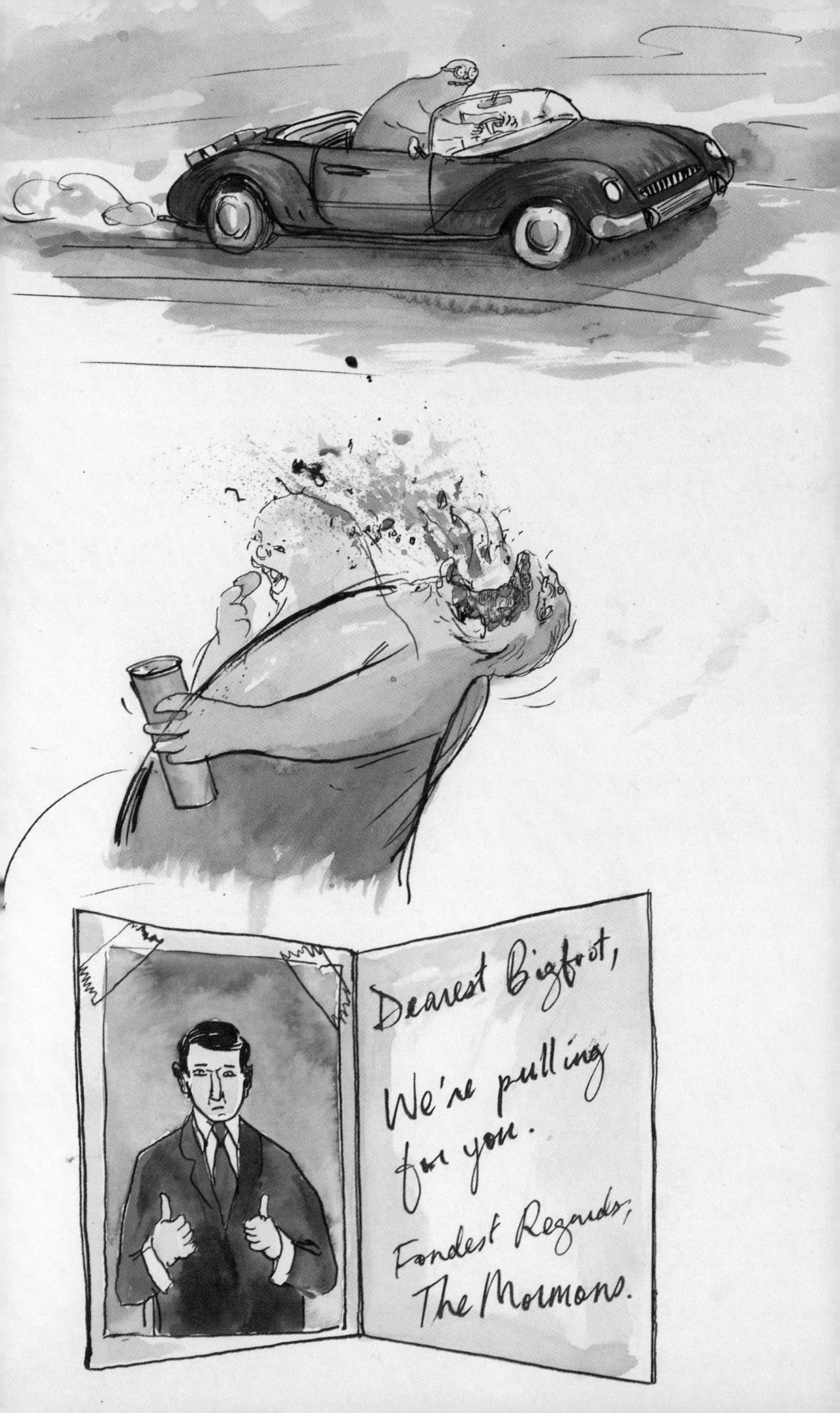
Dearest Bigfoot,
We're pulling for you.
Fondest Regards,
The Mormons.

Let Me Be You Tamagotchi

So I not get much play lately.
Try meet ladies in bar but no so good.
See a piece of whistle bait and Bigfoot make move
Me pretty smoove.
Go to Jukebox, put on Whitesnake
nod along to 'here I go again on me own'.
Check fly, check mouth stink, order two white russian
and saunter over.
I say: 'hello, this seat take?'
Most time lady just run, scream, sometime
pepperspray.
Worst is when they do silent scream and
vomit trickle down chin like hot fudge on
Sundae.
How a guy supposed recover from that?
One time girl friendly let Bigfoot sit.
I figure things good to go so I mark
her with musk so other suitor know.
"Stay Away, She Bigfoot!" No Good!
She allergic to Bigfoot stink and go
into anaphalaxis. Now me on to
web personals, Bigfoot write clever. Read→

FIGBOOT_2001

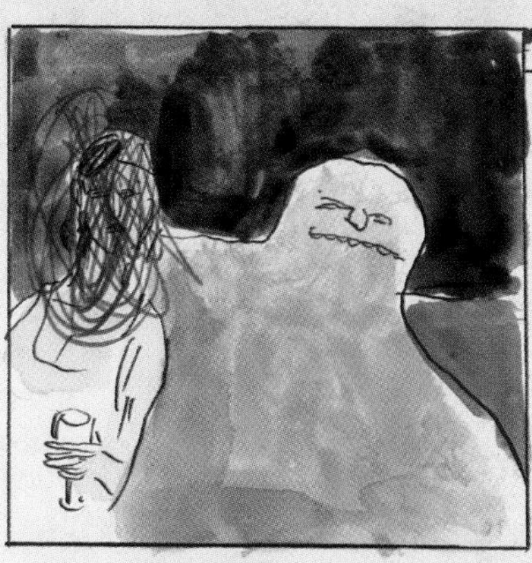

"LET ME BE YOU TAMAGOTCHI"

SEX: ALPHA MALE, JR. SILVERBACK
ETHNICITY: BIGFOOT / NATIVE AMERICAN
LOCATION: NEXT TO CRANBERRY BUSH + STUMP
EDUCATION: DEVRY
LOOKING FOR: HOT SHEFOOT
OCCUPATION: FOREST GENTLEMAN

HEIGHT: 7'1"
WEIGHT: LOTS
EYES: SMALL
HAIR: MATTED, BROWN, GREEN, MARIGOLD
RELATIONSHIP STATUS: SAD AND LONELY
WANT CHILDREN: SMALL LITTER

ACTIVITIES: JAZZERSCIZE, T-BALL DISEMBOWELING, TAXIDERMY, RUNNING FROM CAMERAS, FILTH HOARDING, CHILLIN', CRYING SELF TO SLEEP.

CELEBRITY I MOST RESEMBLE: GOD DAMN CHEWBACCA, MALCOLM JEMAL WARNER, ME SELF, COUSIN IT FROM ADDAMS FAMILY

IF YOU COULD BE ANYWHERE RIGHT NOW: DOLLY PARTON'S UTERUS, ON A BEACH IN THAILAND READING SARTRE SO ME CAN BE DIPSHIT STEREOTYPE HIPSTER LIKE EVERYONE ELSE ON HERE. AT SIX FLAGS EATING FIVE CORN DOGS BY FOUR PORT-A-JOHNS AT THREE IN THE AFTERNOON ON SECOND DAY OF JANUARY.

WHY YOU SHOULD GET TO KNOW ME: HEY I LIKE EASY GOING GUY, KNOW HOW TO HAVE GOOD TIME BUT CAN ALSO BE SEXY AS ALL GET OUT. GIVE GOOD BACK RUBS, SOME-TIME MIGHT CRACK RIB BUT THAT NOTHING BOTTLE OF CHAMPALE IN BUBBLE BATH NO FIX. I PRETTY CLEAN GUY TOO, FAMILY OF VOLES IN ARMPIT TAKE CARE OF BIGFOOT LICE, EARWIG, SILVERFISH, DUNG BEETLE, NITS, GNATS, EARTHWORM, TAPEWORM, GARTER SNAKE, WASP NESTS, ANT COLONY, TERMITE MOUND, CRABS, SCABS, SCABIES, SHINGLES, FOOD BITS SHIT BITS, DINGLEBERRIES, PINK EYE, GREEN EYE AND SO ON. I SMELL LIKE COMPOST BUT COMPOST SMELL LIKE FALL AND FALL VERY NICE WITH PRETTY LEAVES AND PUNKIN' PIE SO YOU JUST VISALIZE THAT AS YOU DRY HEAVE AND EVERYTHING BE OK.

MOST HUMBLING MOMENT: ONE TIME I WALKING DOWN RED CARPET AT FOREST CREATURE AWARDS AND I STEP IN DOG DOO. IF THAT NOT BAD ENOUGH SOME REPORTER THINK HE FUNNY AND SAY "YOU REALLY PUT YOU BIGFOOT IN IT NOW BIGFOOT!" SO I DO WHAT SEEM LIKE RIGHT THING AT TIME AND TEAR HIM HEAD OFF AND USE TO CLEAN FOOT. THEN I REMEMBER I NOMINATED FOR GOOD CITIZEN AWARD FOR ME WORK WITH KID WHAT WEAR HOCKEY HELMET ALL TIME. WHAT A PICKLE, WHAT A PICKLE.

No Touch

Almost every day someone come
up to Bigfoot and ask "Sign this?"
or say they love Bigfoot in last role.
Used to be real big kick.
Something change though, something
in people voice, something about
look in they eye. You all a bunch
of predator. It like you think
Bigfoot owe you something.
Stop trying talk and touch
Bigfoot, you suffocating me.

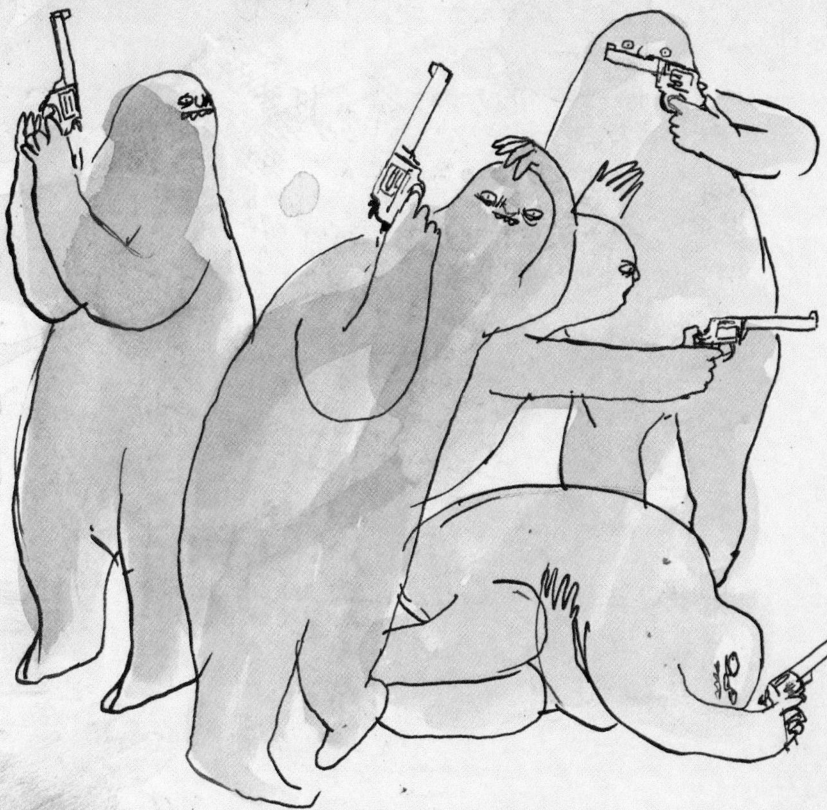

Recently Bigfoot buy gun and fortify home with deep pit and fence of pointy stick. Hire Mr. T as body guard but he startle Bigfoot and I accidently shoot him. He pitying fool in heaven now.

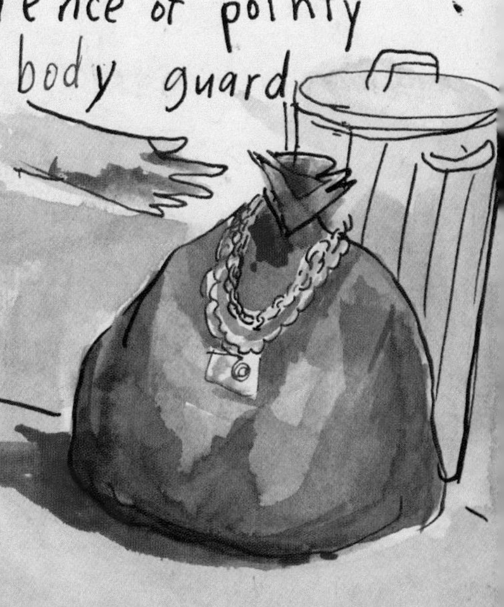

illegitimate

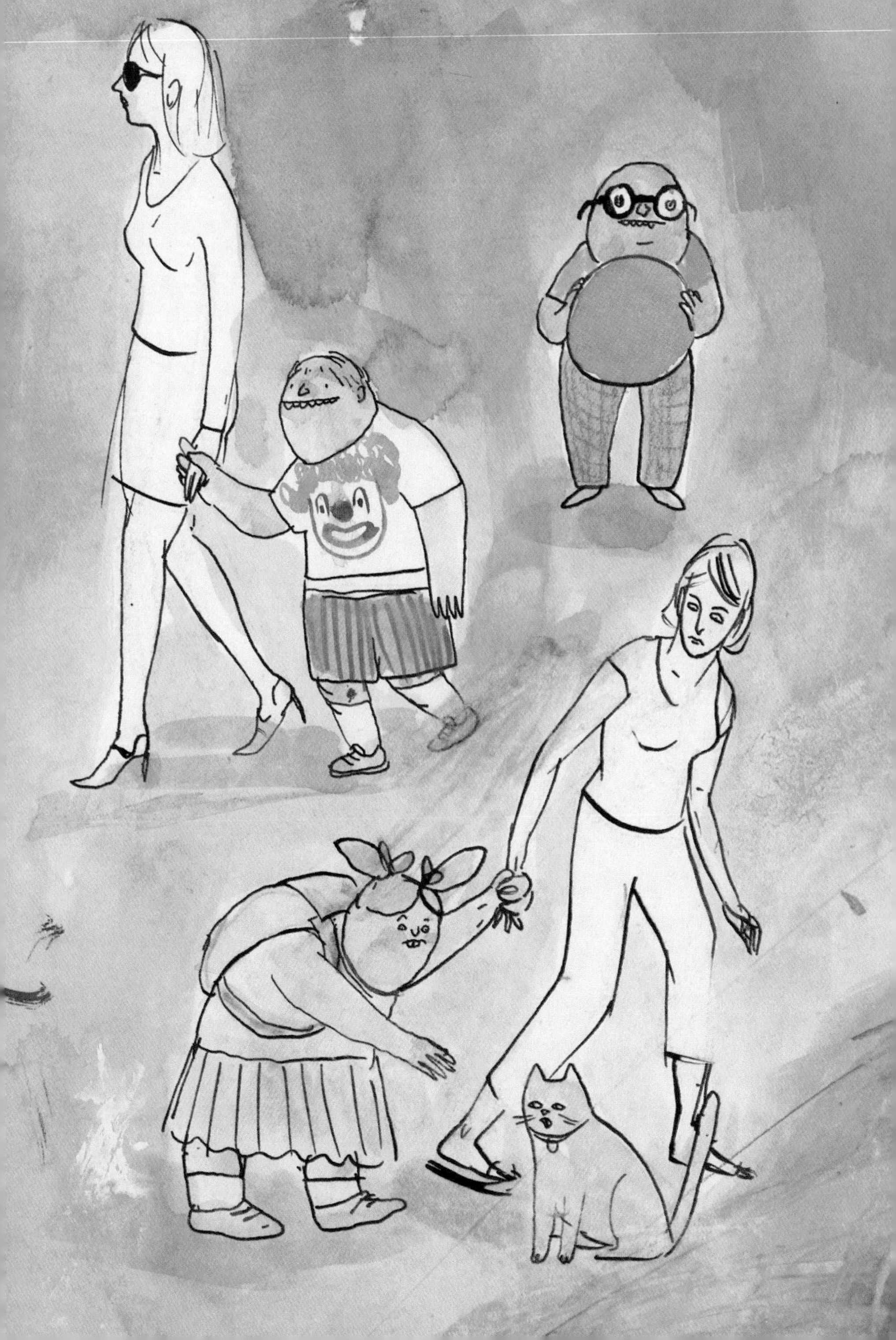

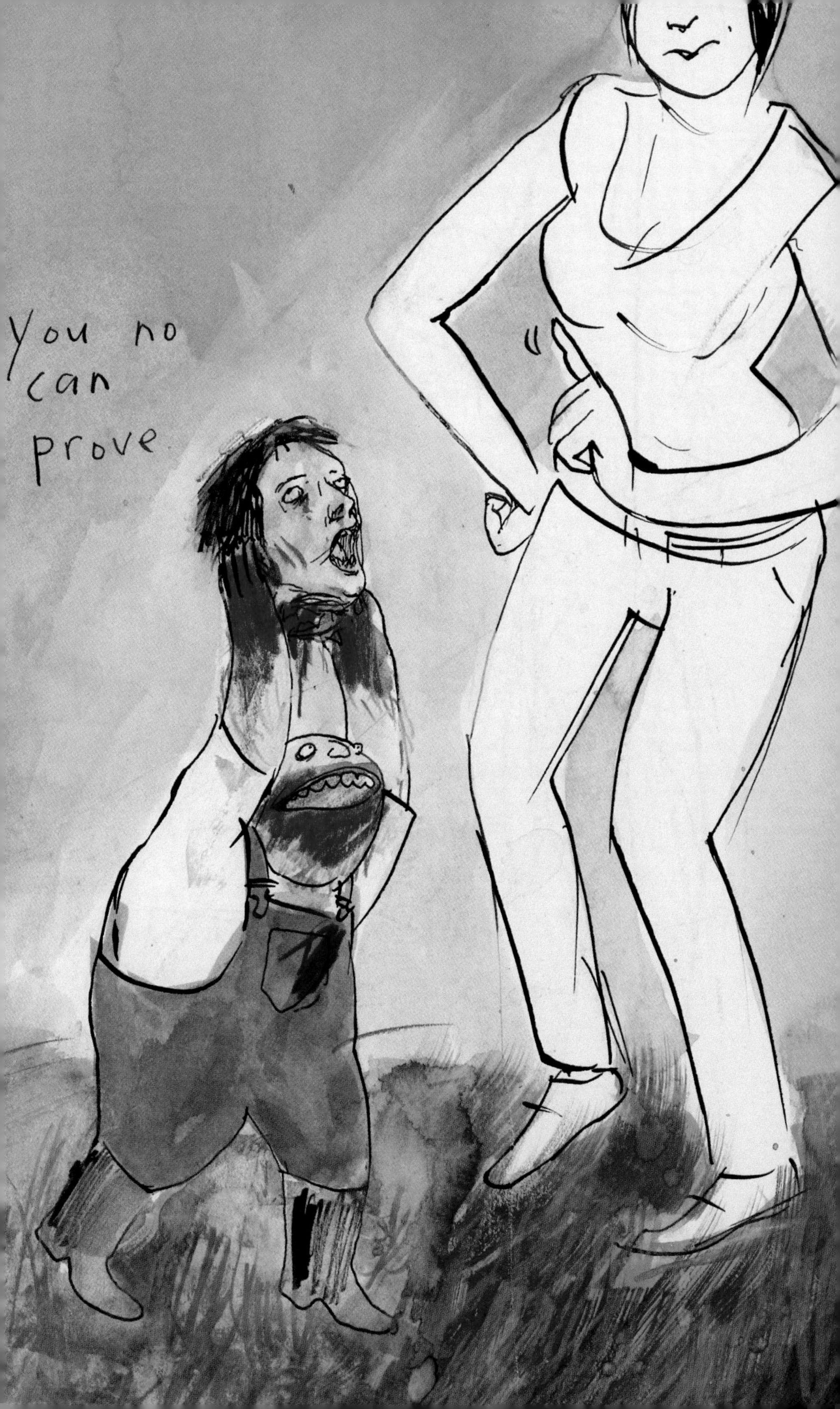
you no can prove

Getting Up There

I suppose it no secret that
Bigfoot no spring chicken.
Full of ache and pain and crickety crack
Make think maybe I no live forever.
Fill toilet to rim with blood other day
Maybe think I look into that,
   Have feeling ladies not dig.

Not old enough for one of those
'Help I fall down and no can get up"
necklaces so instead have elderly man
check upon me using walkie talkie
   in exchange for two minute of
   Companionship a week.

   Some time he be such a drag.
   Thankfully haven't hear from
      him in weeks.

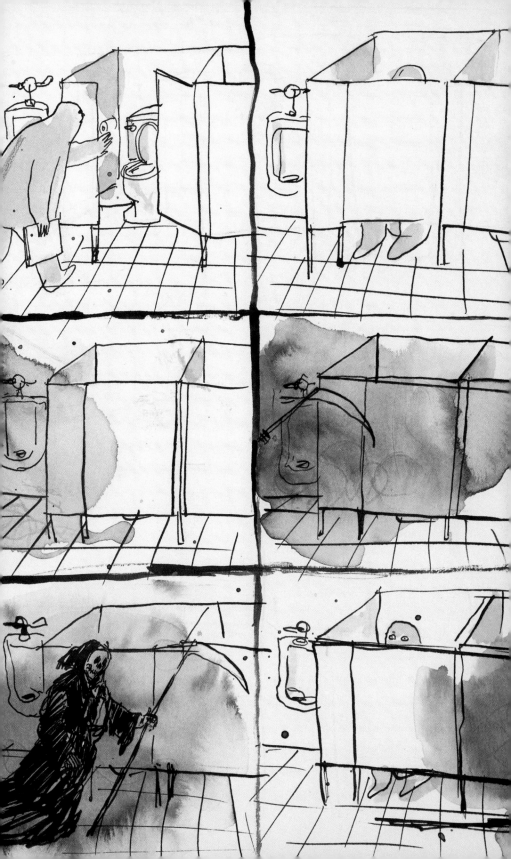

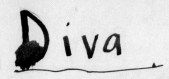

Diva

BIGFOOT TECHNICAL MANUAL
APPENDIX A

!. THE FOLLOWING ITEMS ARE TO BE SET UP IN THE PRINCIPAL ARTIST'S DRESSING AREA:

-one sack of filth (please no domestic filth)

-one heap of assorted shiny objects (no sharp edges please)

-an empty room for yelling adjacent to the artist's primary dressing
 area.

-Bits of beef jerky cleverly hidden to allow for games of 'Hide and Go Beef Jerky'.

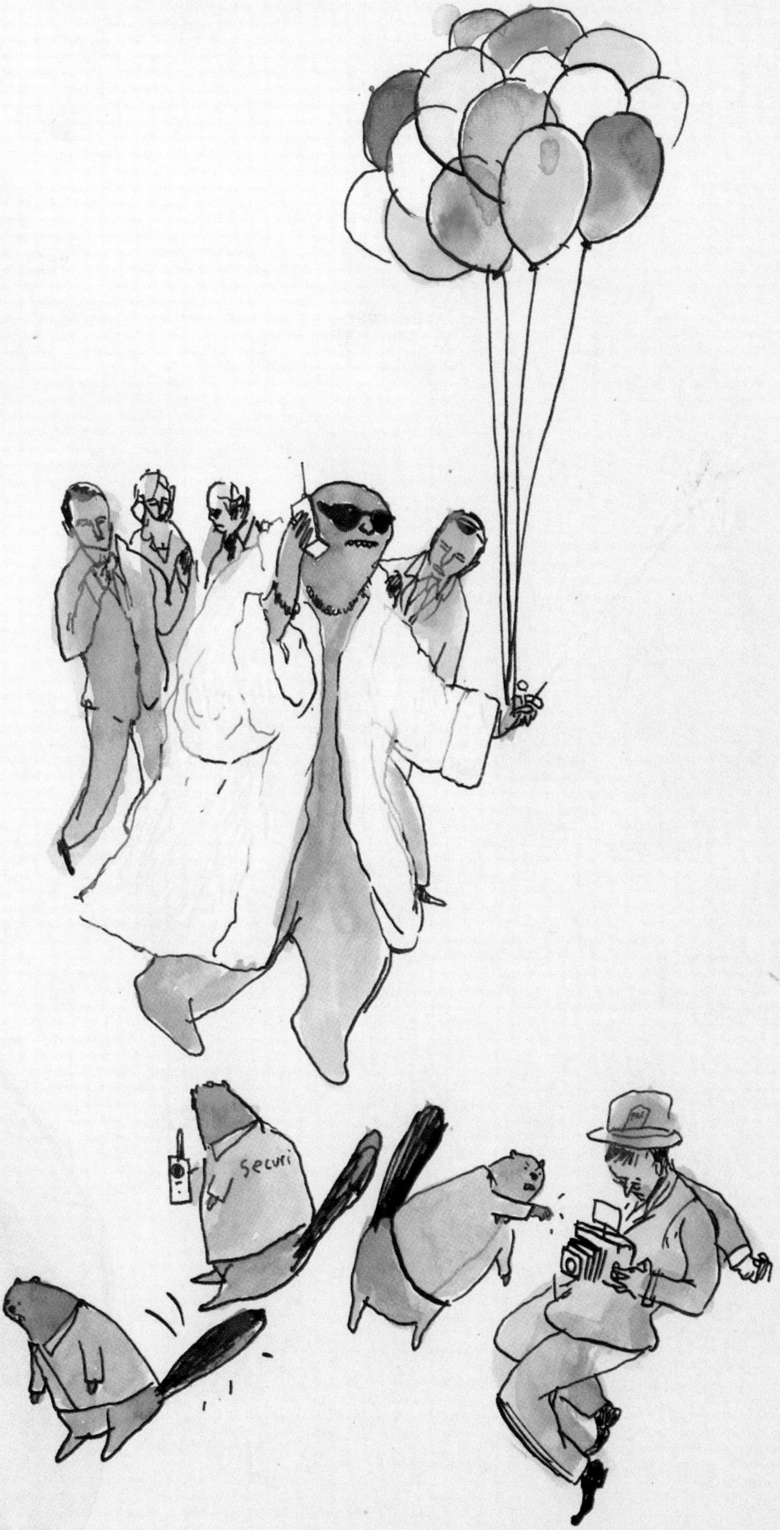
securi

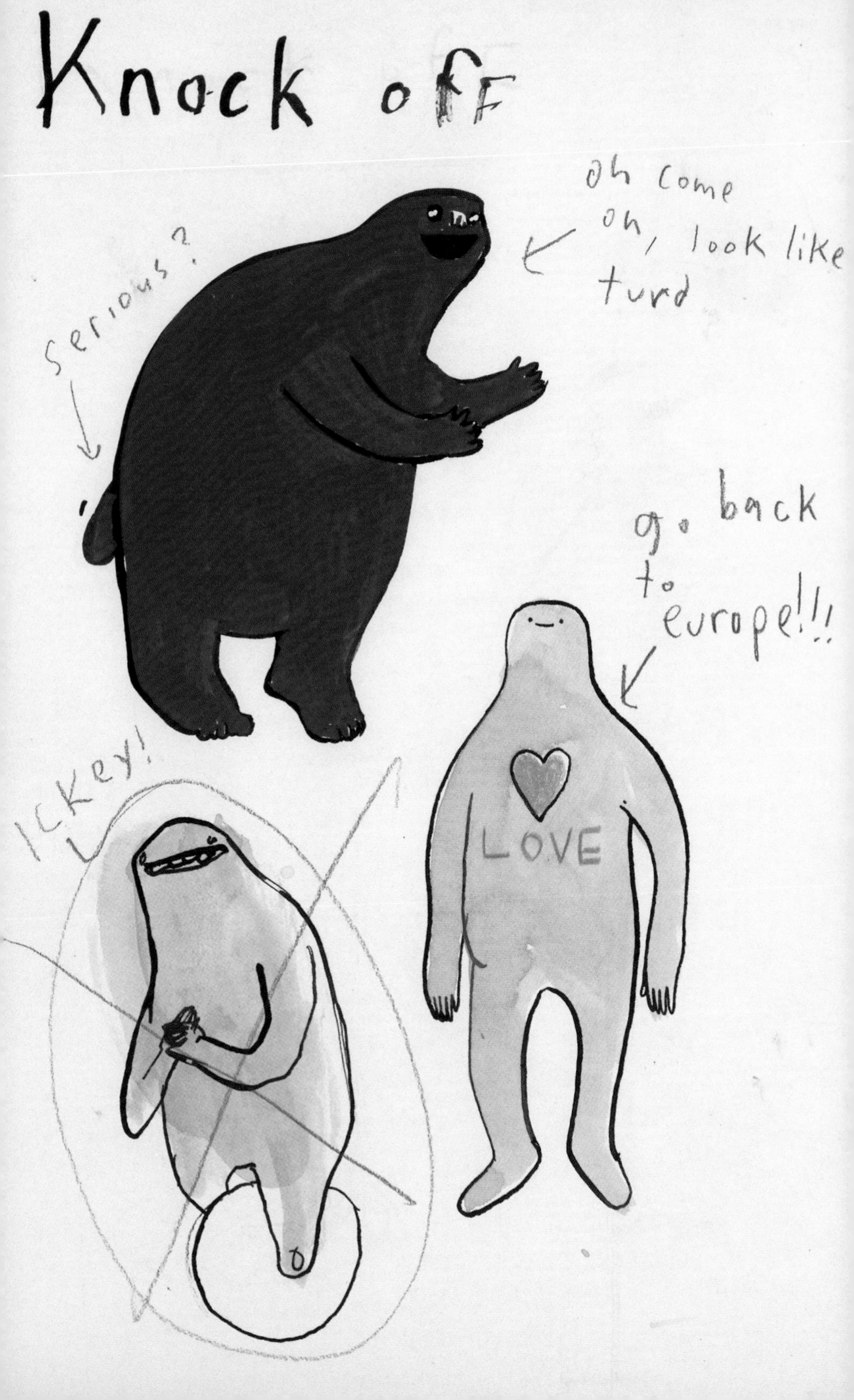

Knock off
oh come on, look like turd
serious?
go back to europe!!!
LOVE
ickey!

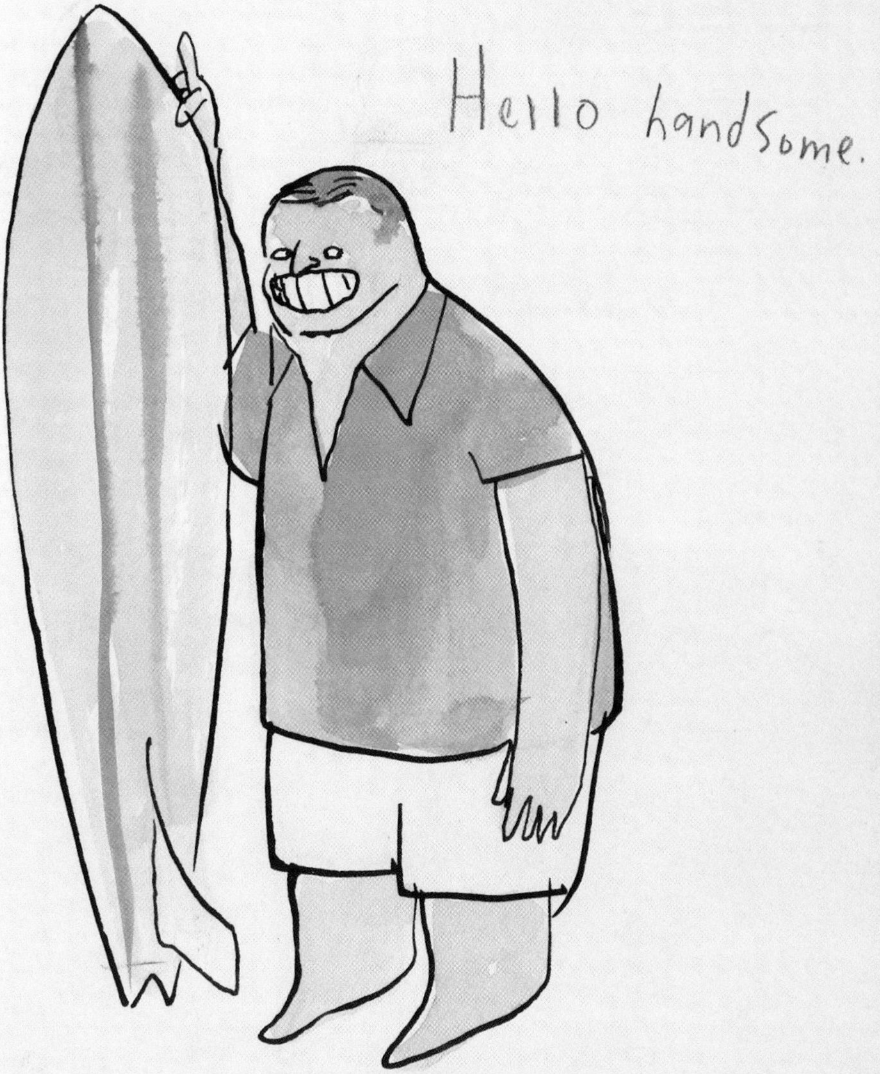
Hello handsome.

Not real Bigfoot. Fake. Everyone want piece of my pie.

LEGACY

"In Bigfoot crazy life had little time to pause and reflect. Every once in while though it hit me how far I come. Go from carrion eating, shadow dwelling

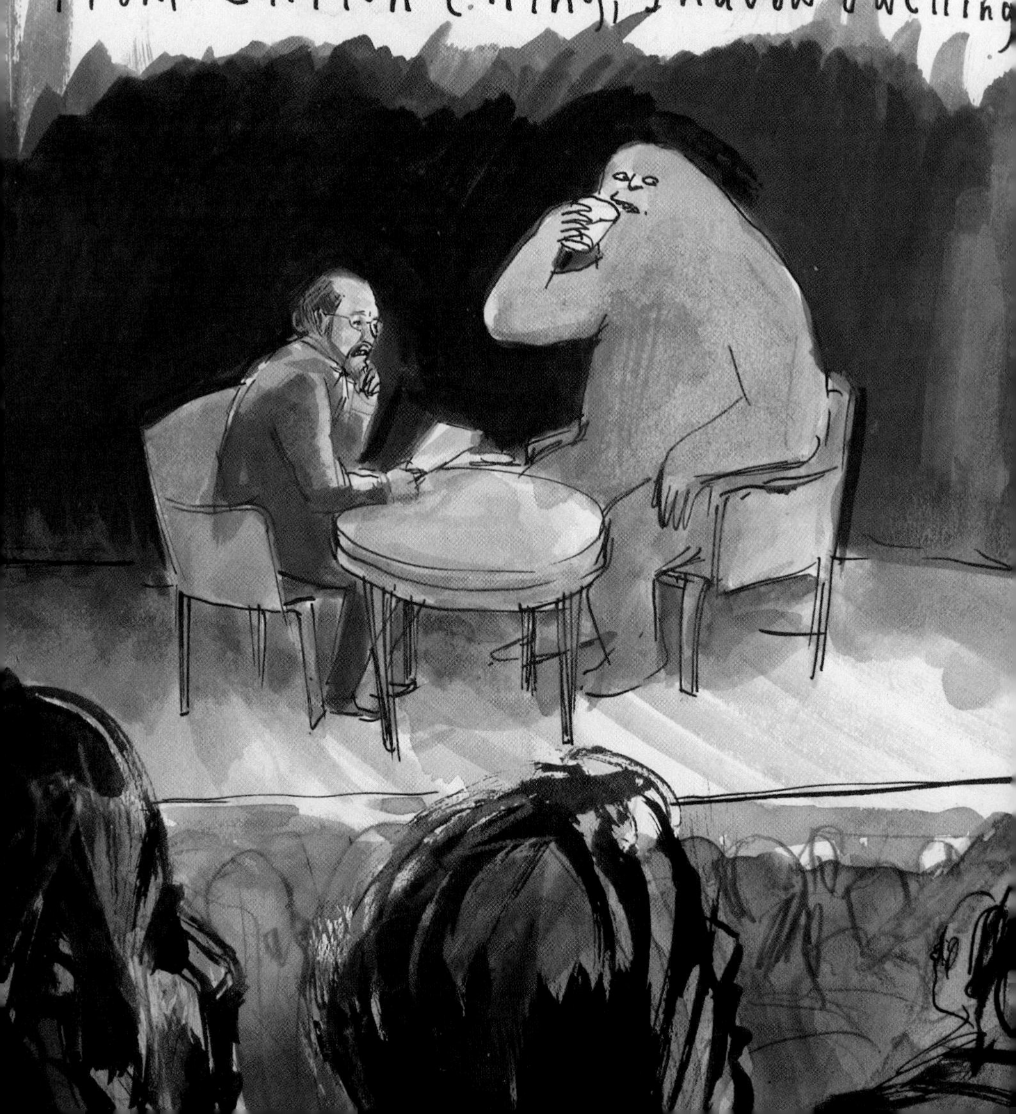

nobody to darling of all media. When young fan come up to Bigfoot and say 'You inspire, want be just like you!,' it warm me heart. Then I reach into pocket, pull out fist size rock and smash they skull in.

No want the competition.

It a tough world, Junior."

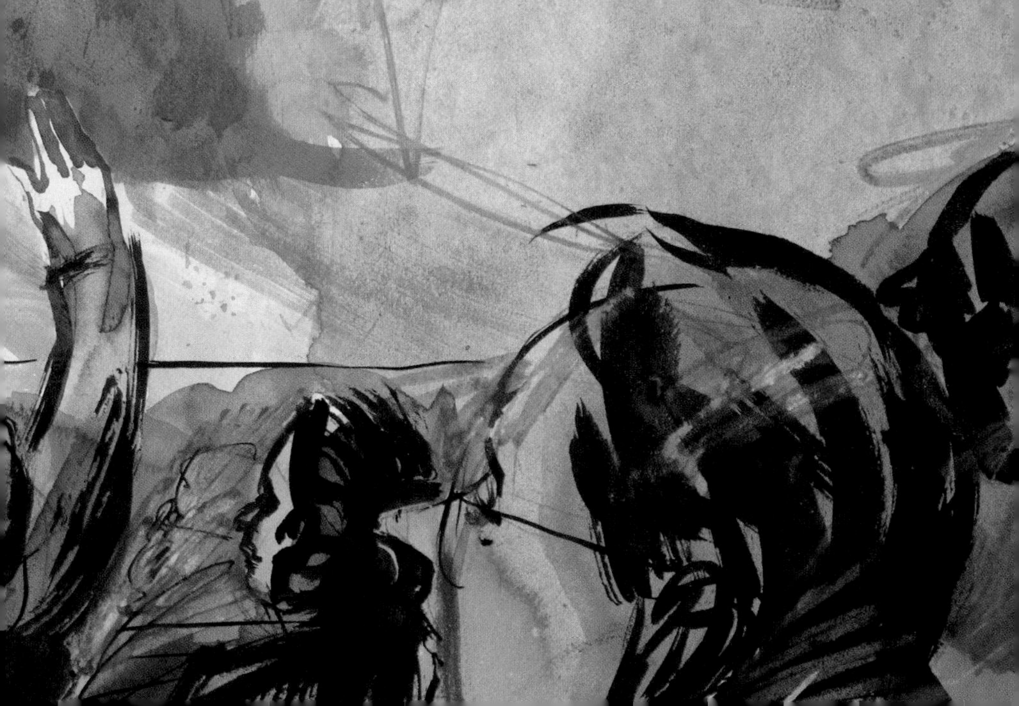

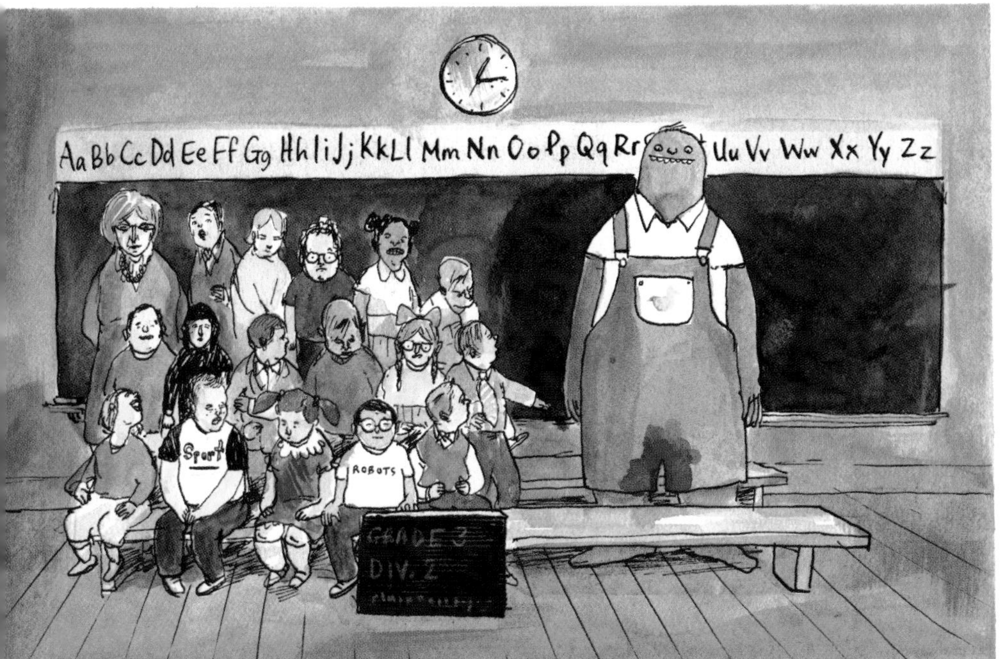
Aa Bb Cc Dd Ee Ff Gg Hh Ii Jj Kk Ll Mm Nn Oo Pp Qq Rr
Uu Vv Ww Xx Yy Zz
Sport
ROBOTS
GRADE 3
DIV. 2

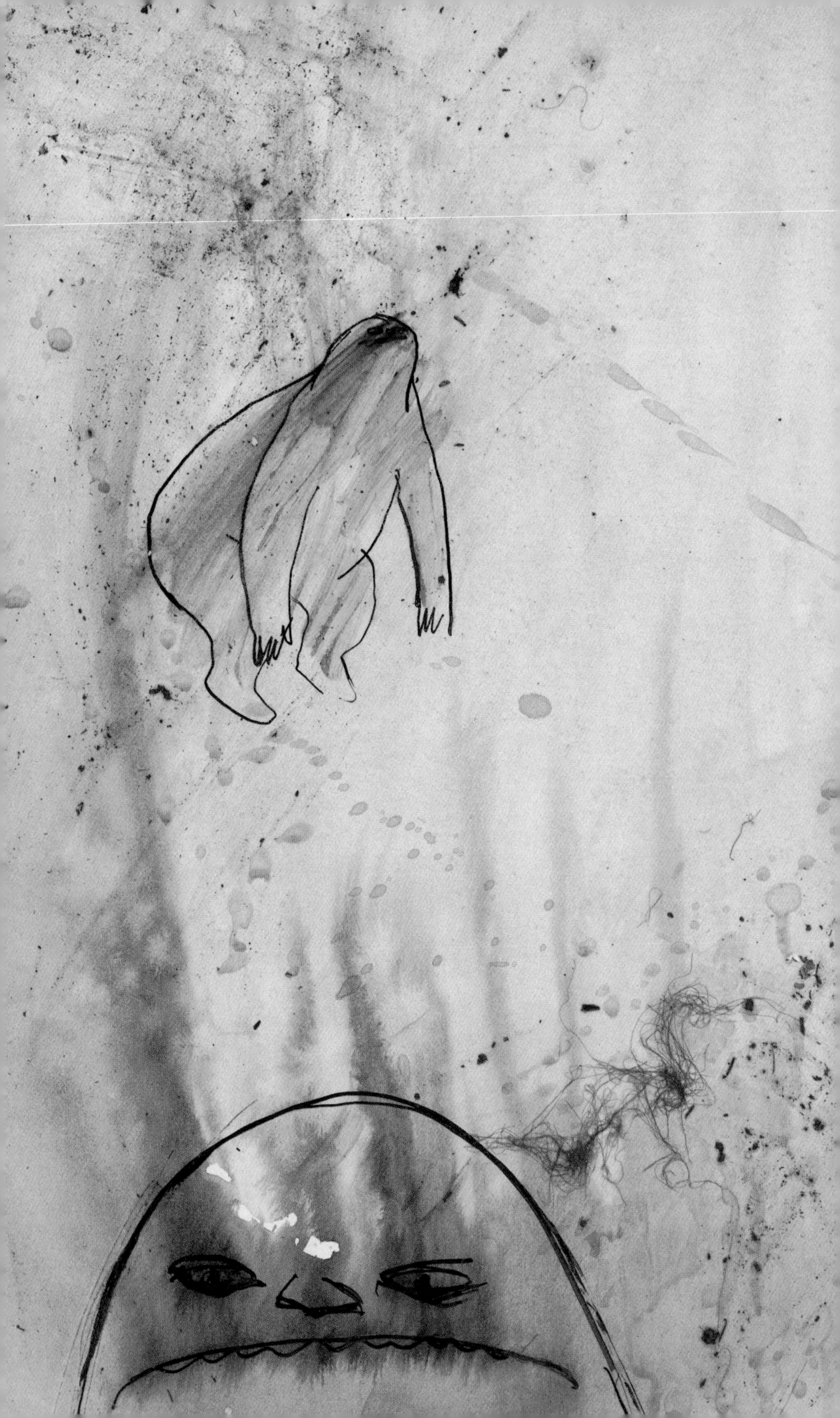